PLAY GAMES WITH ENGLISH

3

TEACHER'S RESOURCE BOOK

COLIN GRANGER
with illustrations by John Plumb

Revised edition in 3 levels

Other photocopiable titles in this series include:

Play Games with English 1 0 435 25016 7
Play Games with English 2 0 435 25017 5
Play Games with English 3 0 435 25018 3

Word Games with English 1 0 435 25088 4
Word Games with English 2 0 435 25089 2
Word Games with English 3 0 435 25090 6

English Sketches 1 0 435 26394 3
English Sketches 1(Cassette) 0 435 26395 1
English Sketches 1 (CD) 0 435 26396 X
English Sketches 2 0 435 26397 8
English Sketches 2 (Cassette) 0 435 26398 6
English Sketches 2 (CD) 0 435 26399 4

Grammar Activities 1 0 435 25094 9
Grammar Activities 2 0 435 25095 7

Ready-made English 1 0 435 24168 0
Ready-made English 2 0 435 24169 9

English Puzzles 1 0 435 25084 1
English Puzzles 2 0 435 25085 X
English Puzzles 3 0 435 25086 8

Macmillan Heinemann English Language Teaching, Oxford
A division of Macmillan Publishers Limited

Companies and representatives throughout the world

ISBN 0 435 25018 3

© Colin Granger and John Plumb 1995
Design and illustration © Macmillan Publishers Limited 1998

Permission to copy
The material in this book is copyright. However, the publisher grants permission for copies of pages to be made without fee on those pages marked with the PHOTOCOPIABLE symbol.

Private purchasers may make copies for their own use or for use by classes of which they are in charge; school purchasers may make copies for use within and by the staff and students of the school only. This permission does not extend to additional schools or branches of an institution, who should purchase a separate master copy of the book for their own use

For copying in any other circumstances, prior permission in writing must be obtained from
Macmillan Publishers Limited.

Cover designed by Martin Cox
Illustrations and student's pages designed by John Plumb

Printed in Great Britain by Athenæum Press Ltd, Gateshead, Tyne & Wear

98 99 00 01 02   12 11 10 9 8 7 6 5 4 3

CONTENTS

TEACHER'S INTRODUCTION	5
INSTRUCTIONS QUIZ	6

Imperative *Keep straight on. Don't overtake yet.*

Instructions Quiz extension — 6
Imperative

Mime Game — 6
Imperative *Come here, please*

CATEGORIES 1 — 8

Adjectives *freezing, cool, boiling*

Categories 1 extension — 8
Adjectives *(Describing people) old, heavy, slim*

Description Game — 8
Adjectives *(Describing objects) It has got a long stick.*

SPOT THE DIFFERENCE 1 — 10

More/As many/As much + Countable/Uncountable Nouns *There are more envelopes. There is more rubbish. There aren't as many stamps. There isn't as much paper.*

What's Different? — 10
As many/As much + Countable/Uncountable Nouns *There aren't as many paper-clips. There isn't as much water.*

OBSERVATION 1 — 12

Want + Object Pronouns + To Infinitive *She wants him to buy her an ice cream.*

Mime Game — 12
Want + Object Pronouns + To Infinitive *I want you to write your telephone number.*

SPOT THE DIFFERENCE 2 — 14

Past Perfect Simple *Somebody had turned on the TV.*

Invention Game
Past Perfect Simple *I'd just stepped on her foot.*

CONNECTIONS 1 — 16

Present Perfect Simple *I've lost my car keys.*
Past Simple *They were in my bag.*

News Quiz — 16
Present Perfect Simple *Someone I know has grown a moustache.*
Past Simple *It took him weeks to grow.*
Present Tenses *He thinks he looks much more handsome with it.*

CONNECTIONS 2 — 18

Adverbs of Manner *'Shut up!' she said angrily.*

Inventions Game — 18
Adverbs of Manner *My son writes very well.*

Charades — 18
Adverbs of Manner *Are you driving fast?*

OBSERVATION 2 — 20

Present Continuous + Prepositions of Movement *Who is falling into the lake?*

Picture Search — 20
Present Continuous + Prepositions of Movement *Someone is coming into a room.*

CONNECTIONS 3 — 22

Compound Nouns *a traffic jam*

Connections 3 extension — 22
Compound Nouns *babysitter*

MEMORY 1 — 24

Past Simple *He stopped on top of the steps.*
Past Continuous *It was getting dark.*
Past Perfect Simple *The bus had left.*

True or False? — 24
Past Simple
Past Continuous
Past Perfect Simple
Past Perfect Continuous

CONNECTIONS 4 — 26

Going to *I'm going to post these letters.*
Will *Don't worry, I'll answer it.*

Choices — 26
Going to (Decisions) *You're going to travel to Paris.*

Inspiration! — 26
Will (Decisions) *I know what I'll do! I'll hitch a lift.*

ING OR -ED? — 28

Participle (-ing and -ed) Adjectives *The book was very interesting. I'm bored.*

Voting Game — 28
Participle (-ing and -ed) Adjectives *I hope you don't find me boring. / I'm bored with this game. Let's play something else.*

CONNECTIONS 5 — 30

Verb + Prepositions *I think I'm going to apply for this job.*

Connections 5 extension — 30
Verb + Prepositions *I don't agree with his political views.*

MEMORY 2 — 32

Future Continuous *You won't be sitting at your desk in the office.*

A Great Day Out — 32
Future Continuous *What will you be doing at 5 pm on Sunday?*

WORD BLUFF — 34

Relative Clauses (Defining) (Who/Where/Which/Whose)
*A teetotaller is someone who never drinks alcohol.
A warehouse is a place where goods are stored.
A saw is a tool which you use to cut wood or metal.
A widower is a man whose wife is dead.*

Word Bluff extension — 34
Relative Clauses (Defining) (Who/Where/Which/Whose)

Star Quiz — 34
Relative Clauses (Defining) (Who/Whose) *Is it the actor who died recently?*

OBSERVATION 3 — 36

Was going to *Someone was going to shave.*

Invention Game — 36
Was going to *I was just going to do it when I noticed that I didn't have the right books.*

PERSONALITY QUIZ — 38

Adjectives *sociable*

Who Is It? — 38
Adjectives *She's got long, dark hair. She's kind and helpful to other people.*

Harry — 38
So/Too + Adjectives *We like Harry because he's so active. We hate Harry because he's too aggressive.*

MEMORY 3 — 40

Reflexive Pronouns/Past Continuous *She was looking at herself in a mirror.*

Mime Game — 40
Reflexive Pronouns/Present Continuous *You're looking at yourself in the mirror.*

THE WORD ORDER GAME 1 — 42

Word Order; Reflexive Pronouns; Conjunctions *He hurt himself quite badly while skiing in Switzerland.*
Comparison of Adverbs *You won't pass the examination unless you work harder.*

Records Game — 42
Comparison of Adverbs *She can see the furthest. She can see further than him.*

DIFFERENCES 1 — 44

Verbs; Vocabulary *Don't go in there. Come here.*

Differences 1 extension — 44
Verbs; Vocabulary *look, see*

MEMORY 4 — 46

Present Simple *I work in a fast food restaurant in Los Angeles.*

CONTENTS CONTINUED ...

Present Continuous *I'm staying with a friend called Annie.*
Present Perfect Simple *I've known Annie for two years.*
Past Simple *I moved to Washington, DC when I was 12.*

Memory 4 extension — 46
Present Simple *Do you smoke?*
Present Continuous *Where are you living at the moment?*
Present Perfect Simple *How long have you worked for the International Bank?*
Past Simple *When did you move to Rome?*

CONNECTIONS 6 — 48
Adjectives + Prepositions *I'm afraid of spiders.*

Connections 6 extension — 48
Adjectives + Prepositions *She gets very anxious about being near a dog.*

MEMORY 5 — 50
Past Perfect Continuous *Because she had been swimming.*

Long Sentence Game — 50
Past Perfect Continuous *She'd been typing letters all day.*

SPOT THE DIFFERENCE 3 — 52
Passive (Present Perfect) *The front door has been mended. Curtains have been put up.*

What's Different? — 52
Passive *Has been done. The board has been cleaned.*

MEMORY 6 — 54
Past Perfect Simple *You had just got on the bus.*
Past Continuous *You were just getting on the bus.*
Was going to *You were just going to get on the bus.*

Memory 6 extension — 54
Past Perfect *You had just stood up.*
Past Continuous *You were reading a book.*
Was going to *You were just going to do some work.*

THE WORD ORDER GAME 2 — 56
Word Order
Adverbs of Frequency *Have you ever been to New York?*

The Word Order Game 2 extension — 56
Word Order

MEMORY 7 — 58
Reported Speech *The announcement said all passengers to Lagos should go immediately to Gate Five.*

Bush-Telegraph — 58
Reported Speech *You said you didn't feel very well.*

CLOSE UPS — 60
Have something done *He's having his hair dyed.*

Invention Game — 60
Have something done (or Get something done) *I need to have the brakes adjusted.*

OBSERVATION 4 — 62
Passive (Past Perfect) *Rock'n'roll hadn't been thought of yet.*

Observation 4 extension — 62
Passive *Had been done. The Arc de Triomphe hadn't been built yet.*

CONNECTIONS 7 — 64
Phrasal Verbs *Who is Danny going out with?*

Drawing Game — 64
Phrasal Verbs *throw away, look forward to, grow up*

TRUE OR FALSE? — 66
Comprehension

True or False? extension — 66
Comprehension

DIFFERENCES 2 — 68
American and British English; Vocabulary *car, automobile*

What Are They Talking About? — 68
American and British English; Vocabulary *faucet, tap*

OBSERVATION 5 — 70
Should have done *He should have cleaned his rifle.*

Long Sentences Game — 70
Shouldn't have done *You shouldn't have drunk so much.*

Invention Game — 70
Should have done *You should have driven more slowly.*
Shouldn't have done *You shouldn't have overtaken the lorry.*

DETECTIVE — 72
Must have done *He must have hidden in the cupboard or in the chest.*

Deduction Game — 72
Could have done *The cats could have had very poor eyesight.*
Could have been doing *The man could have been smoking.*

CATEGORIES 2 — 74
Verb + -ing *I enjoy staying in bed.*
Verb + to Infinitive *I refuse to move.*

Invention Game — 74
Verb + -ing *The thief admitted taking the CD player.*
Verb + to Infinitive *What time did you arrange to come?*

PICTURE STORY — 76
Relative Clauses (Non-defining) *Juliette, whose boyfriend Masim is always late, was waiting outside the church at 11 o'clock, when the wedding was to take place.*

General Knowledge Quiz — 76
Relative Clauses (Non-defining) *John Lennon, who was born in Liverpool in 1945, wrote many famous songs.*

MEMORY 8 — 78
Reported Speech (Questions) *She asked him if he had packed the tin opener.*

Long Sentence Game — 78
Reported Speech (Questions) *She asked me how I was.*

OBSERVATION 6 — 80
Wish + Past Perfect *I wish I had put on different shoes.*

Invention Game — 80
Wish/If only + Past Perfect *I wish I hadn't eaten so much.*

MEMORY 9 — 82
Unreal Past Conditionals (Third Conditional) *If she had cooked the chicken more, she wouldn't have got food poisoning.*

I Regret ... — 82
Unreal Past Conditionals (Third Conditional) *Of course, if I hadn't taken the money, I would still be a minister.*

PRONUNCIATION — 84
Pronunciation

Rhyming Couplets — 84
Pronunciation

Voting Game — 84
Pronunciation

MEMORY 1 — 87
MEMORY 2 — 88
MEMORY 3 — 89
MEMORY 4 — 90
MEMORY 5 — 91
MEMORY 6 — 92
MEMORY 7 — 93
MEMORY 8 — 94
MEMORY 9 — 95
INDEX — 96

TEACHER'S INTRODUCTION

In **Play Games With English 3** you will find **40 main games** on the photocopiable students' pages of the book and a further **48 follow-up games** outlined on the accompanying teacher's pages. Please note that you need to photocopy 2 pages for some of the **Memory** games.

Play Games With English 3 can be used in two ways:

- *systematically* Playing each main game in turn with as many of the follow-up games as you think necessary. As the games are graded, you will be providing systematic practice of language structures appropriate to students at a lower intermediate to intermediate level. The **Contents** on page 3 will show you what language points each game practises.

- *selectively* Choosing and playing games to provide additional practice of points you feel your students need extra help with. **The Index of Structure and Language Points** on page 96 will help you to select games to fit your students' needs.

USING LANGUAGE GAMES IN THE CLASSROOM

Most games in **Play Games With English 3** have four stages:

1. *The Rules of the Game*
   Generally, the best way of getting the students to understand how a game is played is not to explain the rules but to play a trial round with the students.

2. *Choosing Sides*
   The games in **Play Games With English 3** can be played in the following ways:

   - *Player A v. Player B* Here each person in the class plays against each other.
   - *Small team v. Small team* Here the class is divided up into a number of small teams.
   - *Team A v. Team B* Here the class is divided into two teams.
   - *You v. the class* Here you (or individual students in turn) play against the rest of the class.

   Some games are best played in one particular way; in others you can be more flexible. If the students organise themselves into teams, make sure that not all the best students end up in the same team.

3. *Playing the Game*
   In games involving team discussion, stress to your students that the working language should, as far as possible, be English.

   Correction
   While the game is being played, any correction of mistakes should be done in as unobtrusive a way as possible so as not to distract from the game.

4. *Follow up*
   The purpose of this stage is to focus the students' attention on the main language points practised in the game. At this stage, any mistakes made during the game can be corrected and any new vocabulary written up.

INSTRUCTIONS QUIZ

Imperative: *Keep straight on. Don't overtake yet.*

Working individually or in pairs, the players have to match the instructions to an instructor. The first player to do this correctly is the winner.

Hints: Make sure that the players fully understand the instructions by asking detailed comprehension questions after the matching task has been completed.

ANSWERS: A6   B9   C1   D3   E2   F8   G4   H7   I5

INSTRUCTIONS QUIZ – extension   **Imperative**

Divide the class into small teams of two to three players. Appoint team secretaries.
The team secretaries, helped by the rest of their team, write a set of instructions which could be said by a different instructor to those on page 7, e.g.

a policeman, a flying instructor, a doctor, a boss, an art teacher, a science teacher, a do-it-yourself instructor, an army officer, a gangleader, a priest.

The instructions are then read out to the rest of the class who have to try to guess who is saying the words.

MIME GAME   **Imperative:** *Come here, please.*

Get the attention of a student and with the use of gestures and mime get him or her to come out and join you at the front of the classroom. At the same time, by pointing to your mouth and with the use of gestures, prompt this student and the rest of the class to supply your words *Come out here, please* or *Come here, please*. Your mime does not have to be very good – the more amateur the mime the more the students will have to use language to guess what you want to say. Nod your head when somebody comes up with the right answer. Then with the use of gestures and mime get the student to sit down. Again get the class to guess what the instruction for this is: *Sit down, please*. Continue in the same way with other instructions, e.g. *Stand up, please, Take your sweater off, please, Switch on the light, please*. Then get the student you have demonstrated the activity with to choose another student to give new instructions to. And so on.

Which instructor is giving which instruction? Write the number in the box next to the correct instruction.

1. keep fit instructor
2. dancing teacher
3. nurse
4. swimming instructor

5. tennis coach
6. driving instructor
7. cookery teacher
8. language teacher
9. theatre director

A. KEEP STRAIGHT ON. LOOK IN THE MIRROR. DON'T OVERTAKE YET. WAIT, NOW PULL OUT. ☐

B. DON'T SPEAK SO LOUDLY. YOU ARE IN LOVE WITH HER. STAND CLOSER. ☐

C. TOUCH YOUR TOES. DON'T BEND YOUR KNEES. KEEP YOUR BACK STRAIGHT. ☐

D. MAKE SURE THE WATER IS THE RIGHT TEMPERATURE. HOLD HER HEAD UP. DON'T BE AFRAID. NOW PLACE HER IN THE WATER. ☐

E. MEN, PUT YOUR LEFT FOOT FORWARD. LEAN BACK ON YOUR RIGHT FOOT. SWING YOUR PARTNER ROUND. ☐

F. DON'T TRY TO TRANSLATE EVERY WORD. LISTEN CAREFULLY. SPEAK AS MUCH AS POSSIBLE. ☐

G. LIE BACK IN THE WATER. DON'T PANIC. KEEP YOUR BODY STRAIGHT. SLOWLY KICK WITH YOUR LEGS. ☐

H. STIR SLOWLY. ADD A LITTLE WATER. DON'T LET IT BOIL. TURN DOWN THE FLAME A BIT. ☐

I. KEEP YOUR ARM STRAIGHT. KEEP YOUR EYE ON THE BALL. DON'T MOVE ABOUT TOO MUCH. ☐

© Macmillan Publishers Limited 1998.

PHOTOCOPIABLE

CATEGORIES 1

Adjectives: *freezing, cool, boiling*

Divide the class into teams of two to three players. Appoint team secretaries.
The team secretaries, helped by the rest of their team, write the adjectives under the appropriate heading. The first team to correctly categorise the words is the winner.

Hints: When the teams read out their answers you could ask them to put each adjective into a sentence which illustrates the meaning of the word. For example:

There was a freezing wind and ice everywhere.
The weather isn't cold, but it is a little cool.

ANSWERS:	Temperature	Texture	Shape	Size	Taste	Colour
	freezing	rough	rectangular	huge	sour	light
	cool	smooth	oval	minute	bitter	bright
	boiling	hard	square	tiny	sweet	pale
	icy	soft	circular	enormous	spicy	dark
	warm	dry	round	large	salty	fluorescent
	chilly	sharp	triangular	massive	bland	dull

CATEGORIES 1 – extension

Adjectives (Describing people): *old, heavy, slim*

Write up the following categories: *age, weight, build, hair colour, personality, looks, height, intelligence, skin colouring.*
Tell the team secretaries to write down the category headings and then, with the help of the rest of their team, write as many adjectives as they can think of under each heading. For example:

Age	Weight	Build	Hair colour	Personality
old	heavy	slim	blond	kind
young	light	thin	dark	generous

Set a ten-minute time limit.
Each team then reads out their lists of adjectives. The team secretaries should cross out any duplicate adjectives on their lists which are read out by another team. At the end the team with the most adjectives left is the winner. Check that the adjectives are appropriate for the heading.

DESCRIPTION GAME

Adjectives (Describing objects): *It has got a long stick.*

Tell the class that you are going to read out a description for them to guess what it is.
Begin to read the description. For example:

It has got a long stick. The stick is usually make of metal and it has got a curved end which forms a handle. The handle is usually made of wood or plastic. On the top of the stick is a metal frame. The frame is covered with material, usually cotton or a synthetic fabric. This material is waterproofed. What is it? (An umbrella)

Divide the class into teams of two to three players. Appoint team secretaries.
The team secretaries, with the help of the rest of their team, have to write a similar description for a different object. Help them with their descriptions if necessary.
Collect all the finished descriptions and begin to read them out. The teams then have to guess what the objects described by the other teams are. Each team has only one guess. They can either interrupt you as the description is being read out or guess at the end when you have finished reading it. The first team to guess what the object is scores 1 point. At the end, the team with the most points is the winner.

Hints: You could extend this game by getting the teams to write descriptions of well-known personalities for the other teams to guess.

CATEGORIES 1

Put these adjectives in the correct category.

fluorescent, chilly, circular, smooth, rectangular, bland, hard, bright, dry, light, soft, massive, dull, round, pale, tiny, bitter, minute, cool, spicy, boiling, salty, sharp, freezing, rough, huge, dark, warm, large, square, sour, oval, icy, sweet, enormous, triangular

Temperature

freezing
....
....
....
....
....
....

Texture

....
....
....
....
....
....
....

Shape

....
....
....
....
....
....
....

Size

....
....
....
....
....
....

Taste

....
....
....
....
....
....

Colour

....
....
....
....
....
....

SPOT THE DIFFERENCE 1

More/As many/As much + Countable/Uncountable Nouns: *There are more envelopes. There is more rubbish. There aren't as many stamps. There isn't as much paper.*

Working individually or in pairs, the players write down the differences between picture A and picture B.
Set a five-minute time limit.
The player with the most correct sentences is the winner.
Hints: After the players have completed the game you could ask them *where* the objects in question are in picture B. For example:

There are more envelopes on the desk. There is more rubbish in the rubbish bin. There aren't as many stamps on the desk.

ANSWERS:	There are more mistakes (in the letter).
	There are more letters (in the in-tray).
	There is more tea (in the cup).
	There is more string (in the drawer).
	There aren't as many files (on the desk).
	There aren't as many pens (in the drawer).
	There isn't as much glue (in the pot).
	There isn't as much money (in the box).

WHAT'S DIFFERENT?

As many/As much + Countable/Uncountable Nouns: *There aren't as many paper-clips. There isn't as much water.*

You will need a large number of different objects for this game, e.g. *coins, bread, water in a glass, material, paper-clips, books, pencils, string, salt*, etc. Make sure that some of these things are **uncountable nouns**, e.g. *bread, water*.
Place the objects on a table or desk.
Divide the class into two teams, A and B.
Ask the players in Team A to look at what is on the table for one minute. Then, without Team A seeing, get Team B to take away, for example, *some of the coins, some of the water in the glass, some of the paper-clips, some of the string*, etc. In all they should change the total amount or quantity of eight objects. Team A then come back to the table and try to say what there aren't as many/isn't as much of. For example:

There aren't as many paper-clips.
There isn't as much water.

Score 2 points for each correct observation expressed in correct English, but only 1 point if the grammar is wrong. Repeat with Team B.
At the end, the team with the most points is the winner.
Hints: You could also play this game to practise *fewer* and *less*:
There are fewer paper-clips.
There is less water.

Spot the Difference 1

Compare the two pictures. Write what is different in picture B.

Use these words:
              letters   string   files   money
      mistakes   tea   pens   glue

There are more envelopes.   *There is more rubbish.*

There aren't so many stamps.   *There isn't so much paper.*

Find eight more differences in picture B.

1. ....
2. ....
3. ....
4. ....
5. ....
6. ....
7. ....
8. ....

© Macmillan Publishers Limited 1998.

PHOTOCOPIABLE

OBSERVATION 1

Want + Object Pronouns + To Infinitive: *She wants him to buy her an ice cream.*

Go through the example with the whole class. Then divide the class into teams of two to three players and appoint team secretaries. Set a ten-minute time limit for the team secretaries, helped by the rest of the team, to complete the sentences with *want him/her/them + to* infinitive of the verbs at the top of the box + the phrases at the bottom of the box. The team with the most correct sentences is the winner.

ANSWERS:	1. She wants him to buy her an ice cream. 2. He wants her to dry him with a towel. 3. She wants him to bring her a bucket. 4. She wants him to help her build a sandcastle. 5. He wants him to throw him the ball. 6. She wants them to show her the magazine. 7. He wants her to pass him a drink. 8. He wants them to fetch him a deckchair.

MIME GAME

Want + Object Pronouns + To Infinitive: *I want you to write your telephone number.*

Tell the class that you are going to mime an action which they have to guess. Write an action on a piece of paper, e.g. *I want you to write your telephone number*. Choose someone to demonstrate the mime with. Mime the action for him or her and the class to guess: *Do you want me to telephone you?* (Shake your head.) *Do you want him to write something?* (Nod your head, but gesture there is more.) *Do you want me to write my name?* (Shake your head.) *Do you want him to write his telephone number?* Say: *That's right*. Continue with other actions, sometimes choosing individual students to demonstrate the mime with and sometimes two or more students so as to prompt: *Do you want us/them ...?* questions. Your mime does not have to be good to do this activity, in fact, the more amateur the mime, the more questions your students will have to ask. Repeat the mime if they are finding guessing difficult and give verbal hints if necessary.

After a while you could get the students to write down ideas for the rest of the class to guess.

Example actions:

I want you to pass me your pens.
I want you to open the window.
I want you to switch on/off the light.
I want you to give me some money.
I want you show me your identity card.
I want you to fetch me my bag.
I want you to get me a drink of water.
I want you to help me clean the board.

OBSERVATION 1

Look at the picture of a beach. What do these children want their parents to do?

Use these words:

bring   buy   dry   fetch   help   pass   show   throw

a bucket   a deckchair   a drink   an ice cream   the magazine   with a towel   build a sandcastle   the ball

1. She wants him to buy her an ice cream.
2.
3.
4.
5.
6.
7.
8.

SPOT THE DIFFERENCE 2

Past Perfect Simple: *Somebody had turned on the TV.*

Go through the example with the whole class. Then, working individually or in teams of two to three players, the players write down the differences between picture A and picture B. Set a five-minute time limit for them to do this. The player/team with the most correct sentences is the winner.

ANSWERS:	Somebody had turned on the TV.
	Somebody had spilt the orange juice.
	Somebody had broken a plate.
	Somebody had opened the cupboard.
	Somebody had eaten all the sandwiches.
	Somebody had drawn a picture on the wall.
	Somebody had tied a little boy to a chair.
	Somebody had taken the flowers out of the vase.

INVENTION GAME

Past Perfect Simple: *I'd just stepped on her foot.*

Prepare a list of prompt situations to elicit past perfect simple forms, for example, *Why did you say 'I'm sorry' to your friend Mary yesterday?* As an example, elicit from the class what possible explanation there could be for this. For example: *I'd just stepped on her foot. I'd been horrible to her. I'd forgotten her birthday.* Also give an example of an inappropriate explanation, e.g. *I'd just given her a sweet.*

Divide the class into teams of two to three players and appoint team secretaries. Explain that the teams have to write an appropriate explanation for the situations you read out to them using the past perfect simple.

Read out the situations. Set a time limit of two minutes after each one for the teams to discuss and for the team secretaries to write down their answers. Explain that they should still try to attempt an answer even if they do not fully understand the situation you have read out as they are not allowed to ask you questions during the game. Also explain that, if they are unable to find an explanation or write down their answer in time they should go on to the next situation as soon as you start reading it.

Possible situations: (Adapt to the knowledge of your class.)

1. Why did you say 'Don't do that again' to your friend Harry yesterday?
2. Why did you say 'Thank you' to your mother yesterday?
3. Why did you say 'Be careful' to an old woman yesterday?
4. Why did you say 'That's terrible' to your friend Susan yesterday?
5. Why did you say 'I promise' to your teacher yesterday?
6. Why did you say 'I hope so' to your friend Bill yesterday?
7. Why did you say 'I can't' to your father yesterday?
8. Why did you say 'That's very nice of you' to your neighbour yesterday?
9. Why did you say 'Don't be stupid' to your friend Tom yesterday?
10. Why did you say 'No, thank you' to your friend Anna yesterday?

Then get the students to read out their answers. Award 1 point for each appropriate response. At the end, the team with the most points is the winner.

Spot the Difference 2

It was Tina's birthday party last weekend. When her mother left the room to get the cake, everything was fine.

But by the time she got back ...

Eight things had happened in picture B. Try to find them.

Use these verbs:

break   eat   open   take out of   draw   spill   tie   turn on

1. Somebody had turned on the TV.
2.
3.
4.
5.
6.
7.
8.

© Macmillan Publishers Limited 1998.

PHOTOCOPIABLE

CONNECTIONS 1

Present Perfect Simple: *I've lost my car keys.*
Past Simple: *They were in my bag.*

Go through the example with the whole class. Then, working individually or in teams of two to three, the players match the people in the pictures with the sentences they are saying. They should then complete the sentences with the present perfect simple or the past simple of the verbs in the box. Set a ten-minute time limit to complete the game. The player/team with the most correct sentences is the winner.

> ANSWERS:
> 1. A I've lost my car keys. They were in my bag.
> 2. H I've bought a new skirt. It only cost £16.
> 3. D I've been to the dentist's. I had two fillings.
> 4. C I've hurt myself. I cut my hand on a tin.
> 5. E I've found a job. I saw a notice in the paper.
> 6. G I've passed my exam. I got 98 out of 100!
> 7. F I've had a big argument with my boyfriend. He said I was stupid.
> 8. B I've broken my glasses. I walked into a wall.

NEWS QUIZ

Present Perfect Simple: *Someone I know has grown a moustache.*
Past Simple: *It took him weeks to grow.*
Present Tenses: *He thinks he looks much more handsome with it.*

Prepare a list of news items with one or two sentences about each one giving more detailed information about the news, e.g. *Someone I know has grown a moustache. It took him weeks to grow. He thinks he looks much more handsome with it.*

Divide the class into teams of two to three players and appoint team secretaries. Explain to the class that they have to guess what news has happened from some information you are going to give them. Give one or two examples before playing the game. Say, for example, *It took him weeks to grow. He thinks he looks really handsome with it*. Then allow time for the teams to discuss what the news could be and for the team secretaries to write down their answer using the present perfect simple.

Play the game, awarding 1 point to teams guessing the correct answer.

Example news items:

Someone I know has just lost her job. She had an argument with her boss and her boss gave her two weeks' notice.
Someone I know has just won a prize in the lottery. It was the first time he'd bought a ticket. He's going to spend the money on a new car.
Someone I know has fallen madly in love. He can't sleep at night since he met her at a party and talks about her all the time.
Someone I know has just had an operation. He had to have a general anaesthetic and he's still in hospital.
Someone I know has just had her flat burgled. They got in a window and took her video and CD player.
Someone I know has just split up with her boyfriend. He was seeing another woman. She's feeling very sad but is pleased that it's all over between them.
Someone I know has just passed his examination. He is really surprised because he only started revising at the last moment.
Someone I know has lost a lot of weight. He was ill for a long time and didn't feel like eating.

Your students could then invent news items for the rest of the class to guess.

CONNECTIONS 1

What are these people saying on the phone? Match the people with the sentences below.

1. I've lost my car keys.
2. I've bought a new skirt.
3. I've been to the dentist's.
4. I've hurt myself.
5. I've found a job.
6. I've passed my exam.
7. I've had a big argument with my boyfriend.
8. I've broken my glasses.

Then complete the sentences.

Use these verbs:							
	buy	cut	have	hurt	find	get	go to
be	break	pass	cost	say	see	walk	lose

1. [A] I ..'ve lost.. my car keys. They ..were.. in my bag.

2. [ ] I .... a new skirt. It only .... £16.

3. [ ] I .... to the dentist's. I .... two fillings.

4. [ ] I .... myself. I .... my hand on a tin.

5. [ ] I .... a job. I .... notice in the paper.

6. [ ] I .... my exam. I .... 98 out of 100!

7. [ ] I .... a big argument with my boyfriend. He .... I was stupid.

8. [ ] I .... my glasses. I .... into a wall.

© Macmillan Publishers Limited 1998.

PHOTOCOPIABLE

CONNECTIONS 2

Adverbs of Manner: *'Shut up!' she said angrily.*

Working individually or in pairs, the players have to decide which speech balloon fits best with which adverb of manner in the list. The player with the most correct sentences is the winner.

Hints: After the class has completed the game you could get individual players to try to read the sentences as suggested by the adverbs (*sadly, kindly, patiently*, etc.).

You could extend the game, with the help of the class, by writing up a list of other adverbs of manner which can describe how someone says something, for example: *laughingly, hesitantly, moodily, wistfully, jokingly, enthusiastically, coolly, nervously, reproachfully, sulkily.*

The players then have to write a sentence for each adverb of manner similar to those given. When they have done this, get the players to read what they have written for each of the adverbs and discuss which sentence best expresses the meaning of the adverb.

> ANSWERS:
> 2. 'Let me help you,' she said kindly.
> 3. 'I don't mind waiting,' she said patiently.
> 4. 'If you're late again you'll lose your job,' she said strictly.
> 5. 'I adore you!' she said passionately.
> 6. 'I've passed my driving test,' she said excitedly.
> 7. 'I won't come,' she said stubbornly.
> 8. 'Please, don't look at me,' she said shyly.
> 9. 'I'm so lonely,' she said sadly.
> 10. 'You couldn't lend me some money, could you?' she said hopefully.
> 11. 'Get out of my way!' she said aggressively.

INVENTIONS GAME

Adverbs of Manner: *My son writes very well.*

Divide the class into teams of two to three players. Appoint team secretaries.

Write up a list of verbs, for example: *write, work, drive, dance, sing, eat*. Explain that the team secretaries, helped by the rest of their team, have to write down as many appropriate adverbs of manner as they can think of for each of the six verb categories. Write up one or two examples for each category to show them what you mean.

Write	**Work**	**Drive**	**Dance**	**Sing**	**Eat**
well	hard	badly	clumsily	loudly	slowly
neatly	lazily	fast	elegantly	well	greedily

Set a ten-minute time limit. Then get each team to read out their lists in turn using a complete sentence, e.g. *My son writes very well. You write very neatly.* As the other teams read out their answers, the team secretaries should cross out any adverbs on their lists which are the same as those read out by the other team. At the end, the team with the most adverbs of manner left is the winner. (Check that all the remaining adverbs are appropriate to the verbs.)

Hints: You could play a further round with new verbs, e.g. *paint, learn, walk, play, dress, sleep.*

CHARADES

Adverbs of Manner: *Are you driving fast?*

Write an adverb of manner on a slip of paper, e.g. *dangerously*. Hand the slip of paper to a player. Explain that he or she must mime the adverb in conjunction with an appropriate verb for the rest of the class to guess. The player perhaps chooses to mime *drive dangerously*. The rest of the class have to ask questions to find out what is written on the slip of paper, e.g. *Are you driving a car? Are you driving fast? Are you driving quickly?* The player doing the mime should answer by shaking or nodding his or her head. The player who guesses the right answer then gets the chance to mime the next adverb for the others to guess, and so on, until everybody has had a turn. Either write the adverbs yourself or, if the players wish, get them to write their own adverbs to mime.

Hints: A variant of this game is where each player in turn goes out of the room while the rest of the class think of an adverb for him or her to guess. The player then comes back into the room and asks questions to find out what adverb the others have chosen.

For example, the class choose *enthusiastically*:

Player:	*Is it a pleasant word?*
Class:	(answer very enthusiastically) *Yes, it is.*
Player:	*Is it a good word for me?*
Class:	(still enthusiastic) *No, it isn't.*

CONNECTIONS 2

How do you think these sentences are said? Connect the sentences with the most appropriate adverb.

For example:

1. '............Shut up...........!' she said angrily.
2. '................................,' she said kindly.
3. '................................,' she said patiently.
4. '................................,' she said strictly.
5. '................................!' she said passionately.
6. '................................,' she said excitedly.
7. '................................,' she said stubbornly.
8. '................................,' she said shyly.
9. '................................,' she said sadly.
10. '................................?' she said hopefully.
11. '................................!' she said aggressively.

© Macmillan Publishers Limited 1998.

OBSERVATION 2

Present Continuous + Prepositions of Movement:
Who is falling into the lake?

Go through the example with the whole class. Then divide the class into teams of two to three players and appoint team secretaries. Set a five-minute time limit for the team secretaries, helped by the rest of the team, to complete the questions with the present continuous of the verbs in the box. The team with the most correct questions is the winner.

ANSWERS:
1. Who's falling into the lake? E
2. Who's jumping across the stream? D
3. Who's swimming under the bridge? C
4. Who's crossing the bridge? I
5. Who's crawling through the tunnel? N
6. Who's climbing up the rope? L
7. Who's sliding down the slope? F
8. Who's lifting a child over the wall? P
9. Who's sitting next to the kiosk? B
10. Who's running towards the kiosk? K
11. Who's cycling away from the kiosk? M
12. Who's standing inside the kiosk? Q
13. Who's lying under a tree? R
14. Who's jogging past the park? H
15. Who's coming into the park? O
16. Who's going out of the park? J
17. Who's chasing somebody around the fountain? G
18. Who's playing in the fountain? A

PICTURE SEARCH

Present Continuous + Prepositions of Movement:
Someone is coming into a room.

Cut out pictures from magazines of scenes involving people, animals and vehicles moving about. For example, people coming out of/going into buildings and rooms. People getting into/on(to)/out of buses, cars, trains, etc. People walking along roads, pavements, etc. People going up/coming down stairs, steps, escalators, etc. People walking across roads, bridges, etc. People or vehicles going under/over bridges. Try to cover all the prepositions introduced in Observation 2. You will need two to three pictures for each student in your class. Choose pictures you can describe with at least two different sentences involving prepositions of movement. For example:

Someone is coming into a room.
Something is climbing into something.

Write two or three sentences describing each picture. Use *someone/something* and prepositions of movement. Try to make each description unique to one of the pictures (i.e. it should only fit one of the pictures in your collection). Write each description on a separate card. Then share out the pictures and cards in random order.

The players first check whether the descriptions on their cards match the pictures they have in their possession. They should then move around the room telling other players their descriptions and swapping pictures with other players. The first player to have matched all his or her cards with the right pictures is the winner.

OBSERVATION 2

Look at this picture of a park and complete the questions below.

Use these words:

chase, climb, come, crawl, cross, cycle, fall, go, jog, lie, jump, lift, swim, play, sit, run, slide, stand

1. Who **'s falling** into the lake? **E**
2. Who .... across the stream? ....
3. Who .... under the bridge? ....
4. Who .... the bridge? ....
5. Who .... through the tunnel? ....
6. Who .... up the rope? ....
7. Who .... down the slope? ....
8. Who .... a child over the wall? ....
9. Who .... next to the kiosk? ....
10. Who .... towards the kiosk? ....
11. Who .... away from the kiosk? ....
12. Who .... inside the kiosk? ....
13. Who .... under a tree? ....
14. Who .... past the park? ....
15. Who .... into the park? ....
16. Who .... out of the park? ....
17. Who .... somebody around the fountain? ....
18. Who .... in the fountain? ....

© Macmillan Publishers Limited 1998.   21

CONNECTIONS 3

Compound Nouns: *a traffic jam*

Go through the example with the whole class. Then, working individually or in teams of two to three, the players match the pictures with compound nouns made up from the lists of nouns. They should then write the nouns under the correct pictures. Set a ten-minute time limit to complete the game. The player/team with the most correct words is the winner.

ANSWERS:		
	1. a traffic jam	10. a tin opener
	2. a nightclub	11. a sports car
	3. a gold ring	12. a greenhouse
	4. a video cassette	13. a shopping bag
	5. a tennis coach	14. a clothes shop
	6. a film star	15. a crossroads
	7. a car key	16. an alarm clock
	8. a taxi driver	17. an oil well
	9. a toothbrush	18. a wool sweater

CONNECTIONS 3 – extension

Compound Nouns: *babysitter*

Write two lists of nouns which together make compound nouns on the board. The lists should be written in jumbled order, for example:

1. baby   driver
2. book   opener
3. bottle   shelf
4. screw   sitter

Divide the class into teams of two to three players and appoint team secretaries. Then go through an example with the whole class. Pointing to the first noun in the list on the left-hand side of the board, get the class to say what noun in the right-hand list can be linked to it to form a compound noun. Then set a ten-minute time limit for the team secretaries, helped by the rest of their teams, to write down a list of compound nouns.

The winner is the team with the most correct answers.

Example list of nouns: (Adapt to the knowledge and level of your class.)

babysitter   drug addict
bookshelf   girlfriend
bottle opener   lawnmower
bus station   screwdriver
ice cream   shoe shop
clothes hanger snowflake
corkscrew   table lamp
daydream   tracksuit
doorknob   waiting room

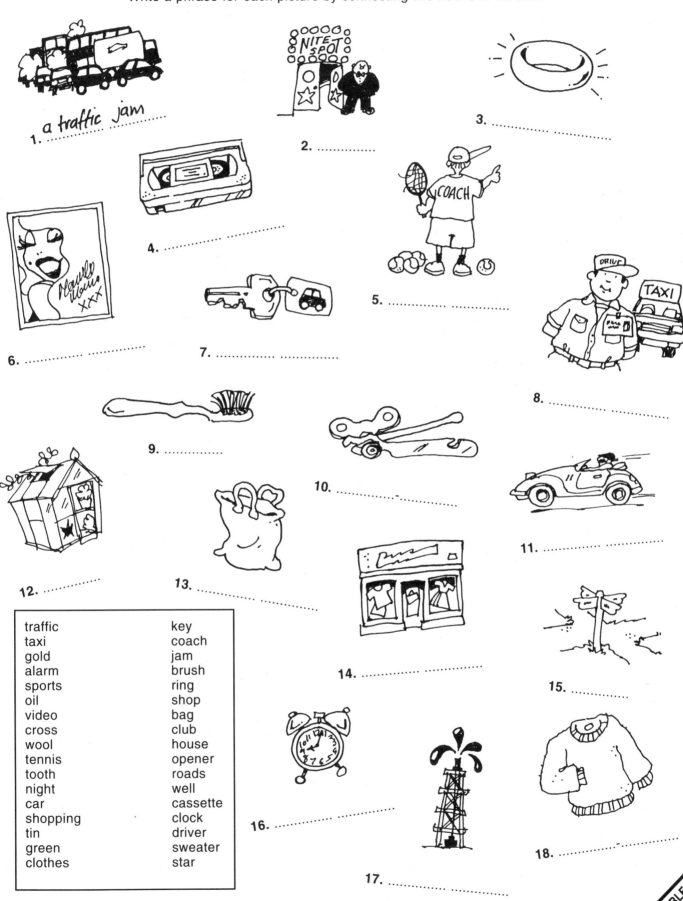

MEMORY 1

Past Simple: *He stopped on top of the steps.*
Past Continuous: *It was getting dark.*
Past Perfect Simple: *The bus had left.*

Photocopy pages 25 and 87 to play this game.

Divide the class into teams of two to three players and appoint team secretaries. Hand out page 25 and give the teams five minutes to study and memorise the picture. Then get the teams to cover or hand you back page 25. Hand out page 87 and go through the example with the whole class. Make it clear that they have to choose between the past simple, the past continuous and the past perfect simple.
The team secretaries, helped by the rest of their team, then write down the answers to the questions. Set a twenty-minute time limit. They must not look back at the first page while doing this. The team with the most correct answers is the winner.

ANSWERS:	It was getting dark when Manolo got out of school. He stopped on top of the steps to speak to a friend. But then he noticed his school bus at the bus stop across the road. He quickly waved goodbye to his friend and ran down the steps and across the road.
	There was a lot of traffic and by the time he got to the other side of the street, the bus had left. He had missed his bus and there wasn't another bus to his village for two hours.
	Manolo looked at his watch: it was five to six and his parents were expecting him home at seven. He was sure they would be very angry. He had to get home somehow by seven.
	Then he had an idea. There was a market a few hundred metres down the road which finished at six. There would be a lot of lorries leaving the market and going down the main coast road past his village.
	When Manolo got to the market, a lorry was pulling out of the entrance. Manolo couldn't believe his luck; it was going to Rosario, a small town just past his village. There was no time to speak to the driver. Manolo climbed into the back as the lorry stopped at the edge of the road to let some cars past.
	Manolo was in the lorry and he was on his way home. When Manolo sat down on the floor of the lorry, he had a big shock. He wasn't sitting on the floor, he was sitting on something very soft. He looked down. It was a large pig. The lorry was full of pigs.
	When Manolo jumped off the lorry in his village, the school bus hadn't arrived. Some parents were waiting at the bus stop for their children.
	Manolo ran up the hill to his house. When he opened the door, his parents were sitting at the table. They smiled when they saw their son. 'You're early, Manolo,' his father said. 'Yes,' replied Manolo, 'but I'm afraid I'm also a bit smelly.'

TRUE OR FALSE?

Past Simple; Past Continuous; Past Perfect Simple; Past Perfect Continuous

Prepare two stories to tell the class. These stories shouldn't take longer than three minutes to tell. Both stories should be about events that happened to you in the past. One story should be true in every detail, while the other should contain things that are exaggerated or untrue. Choose events that were extraordinary in some way, e.g. an amazing coincidence that happened to you. Rather than thinking of an entirely fictitious story, it is easier to base the false story on true events and then distort or exaggerate certain details. Make sure that the stories contain examples of the past simple, the past continuous, the past perfect simple and the past perfect continuous.
Divide the class into pairs. Explain that you are going to tell them two stories and that they then have to decide which story is true and which false. Tell the stories to the class and then give the pairs time to discuss together before getting them to vote on the answer. Then tell the class the answer.
Next, get the pairs to prepare stories to tell the class. Each student tells one story about him or herself. Before preparing their stories, they should first decide whose story is going to be true and whose false. Give some general advice about preparing the stories (see above). Set a time limit for the preparation. Finally, get each pair to tell their stories to the rest of the class. The class then vote on the answer after each pair has completed their stories.

MEMORY 1

Look at this picture story. You have five minutes to memorise it.

Now look at the second page.

© Macmillan Publishers Limited 1998.

CONNECTIONS 4

Going to: *I'm going to post these letters.*

Go through the examples with the whole class. Then, working individually or in teams of two to three players, the players match the people in the pictures with the sentences they are saying. They should then complete the sentences with *going to* or *will* and the verbs in the box. Set a ten-minute time limit to complete the game. The player/team with the most correct sentences wins.

> ANSWERS:
> 1. D I'm going to post these letters.
> 2. H Don't worry. I'll answer the telephone.
> 3. A I'm going to get a coffee. Would you like one?
> 4. E Thanks very much. I'll pay you back tomorrow.
> 5. B Don't lift that box. You'll hurt your back.
> 6. C I'm going to speak to the manager. Wish me luck!
> 7. F I'm going to make spaghetti bolognese tonight.
> 8. G You look hot. I'll switch on the fan.

CHOICES

Going to **(Decisions):** *You're going to travel to Paris.*

Prepare a series of choices based on the level and age group of your students, for example, *travel to Paris/Bangkok, have a cola/an orange juice, get a Volvo/a BMW*.
Explain to the class that they have to second guess what decisions their class colleagues have made using their knowledge of them. Give an example of what you mean. Choose a student and say: *You have the chance to travel to either Paris or Bangkok. Write down which city you want to travel to.* When the student has written down his or her choice, ask the rest of the class to guess what decision he or she has made and write down either: *He/She is going to travel to Paris* or *He/She is going to travel to Bangkok*. Then get the original student to tell them what decision he or she made, e.g. *I'm going to travel to Bangkok.* Continue with other examples, e.g. *Someone offers you a choice of either a cola or an orange juice. Write down which drink you want. You need a new car and have the chance of either getting a Volvo or a BMW at a very good price. Write down the car you want.* Players could award themselves 1 point for every correct guess they make and the winner is the player who makes the most correct guesses.
Example choices:

> Go on a beach holiday/a holiday in the country.
> Wear smart clothes/casual clothes.
> Travel by train/car.
> Write a letter/make a phone call.
> Have a salad/hamburger.

INSPIRATION!

Will **(Decisions):** *I know what I'll do! I'll hitch a lift.*

Prepare a list of prompts to elicit decisions, for example, *I can't get there by bus or by train*. Explain to the students that you are going to read out some problems and that they have to continue with a possible solution to the problems beginning with *I know what I'll do! I'll ... .* Give one or two examples, e.g. *I haven't got any money. I know what I'll do! I'll borrow some from my girlfriend. I'm too tired to concentrate. I know what I'll do! I'll have a black coffee.*
Divide the class into teams of two to three students. Then work round the class, giving individual teams prompts. Give the students one minute for the team to discuss before giving their solution. You could award points for each appropriate response. If a team doesn't understand the prompt or fails to find a solution, give the same prompt to the next team.
Example prompts:

> I'm freezing.
> I keep forgetting things.
> I'm really bored.
> I'm putting on a lot of weight.
> I can't do my homework.
> I've got a sore throat.
> I've lost my purse.

CONNECTIONS 4

What are these people saying? Match the person with the sentences below.

Then complete the sentences. Use these verbs with *going to* or *will*.

| answer | get | hurt | make | pay | post | speak | switch on |

1. [D] I ....*'m going to post*........ these letters.

2. [ ] Don't worry. I ....*'ll answer*........ the telephone.

3. [ ] I .... a coffee. Would you like one?

4. [ ] Thanks very much. I .... you back tomorrow.

5. [ ] Don't lift that box. You .... your back.

6. [ ] I .... Wish me luck!

7. [ ] I .... make spaghetti bolognese tonight.

8. [ ] You look hot. I .... the fan.

-ING OR -ED

Participle (-ing and -ed) Adjectives: *The book was very interesting. I'm bored.*

Go through the example with the whole class. Then, working individually or in teams of two to three, the players write sentences for each picture using adjectives ending in -ing or -ed. The first player/team to complete this correctly is the winner.

> **ANSWERS:**
> 2. I'm bored.
> 3. This film is so exciting.
> 4. Don't be so embarrassing.
> 5. Are you tired?
> 6. You are confusing me.
> 7. I'm too worried to go to sleep.
> 8. This article is really shocking.
> 9. I'm feeling depressed.

VOTING GAME

Participle (-ing and -ed) Adjectives: *I hope you don't find me boring. / I'm bored with this game. Let's play something else.*

Ask each player to write the endings -ing and -ed in large letters on separate pieces of paper. Then write up a list of verbs that can be changed into adjectives by adding -ing or -ed, for example, *bore*, *tire*, *amuse*. Then, as an example, point to the first verb on your list, *bore*, and say *I hope you don't find me ...* Get the class to vote which ending they think correct by holding up one of their voting cards. They should vote in unison and not look at what others are voting before deciding. You might want to cue their votes with a gesture. Then give another example, again pointing at the verb *bore*. *I'm ... with this game. Let's play something else.*

Then start playing the game for real. Players get a minus point if they (*a*) hold up the wrong card; or (*b*) hesitate too long. At the end, the player with the least number of minus points is the winner.

Example verbs and sentences: (Adapt to the level of your class.)

> bore (I hope you don't find me ... . / I'm ... with this game. Let's play something else.
> tire (I don't feel ... . / I've had a very ... day.)
> amuse (I thought the film was quite ... . / I'm smiling because I'm ... .)
> worry (I was ... when you didn't come home. / What the doctor said was ... .)
> interest (It's an ... idea. / I'm not ... in politics.)
> surprise (I'm ... to hear that he's only 25. / The news was ... .)
> shock (Do your parents get easily ... . / Don't say that. It's really ... .)
> embarrass (Why are you ... ? What did I say? / I did something very ... yesterday.)
> depress (The weather is really ... . / I always get ... when it rains a lot.)
> relax ((Hot baths are very ... . / I don't feel ... .)
> annoy (Stop ... me! / Don't speak to her now. She's ... .)
> frighten (I'm ... . Switch on the light. / Don't go and see that film. It's really ... .)
> excite (We're going on holiday. Isn't it ... ? / The children are too ... to go to sleep.)

-ing or -ed?

Choose the correct word to complete the sentences.

1.
interested/interesting

The book was very interesting.

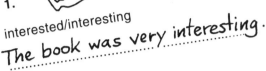

2.
bored/boring

I'm ....

3.
excited/exciting

This film is so ....

4.
embarrassed/embarrassing

Don't be so ....

5.
tired/tiring

Are you .... ?

6.
confused/confusing

You are .... me.

7.
worried/worrying

I'm too .... to go to sleep.

8.
shocked/shocking

This article is really ....

9.
depressing/depressed

I'm feeling ....

CONNECTIONS 5

Verb + Prepositions: *I think I'm going to apply for this job.*

Go through the example with the whole class. Then, working individually or in teams of two to three, players match the pictures with the sentences. They should then complete the sentences with the correct prepositions. Set an eight-minute time limit to complete the game. The player/team with the most correct sentences is the winner.

ANSWERS:
2. G She's apologising to the woman for waking her up.
3. E Do these shoes belong to you?
4. A He's complaining to the manager about his meal.
5. L I can't concentrate on my homework.
6. B What were you dreaming about?
7. C Why are you laughing at me?
8. J I'm listening to the neighbours.
9. F I'm looking for my socks
10. H Can you pay for my drink?
11. I Don't shout at me!
12. D Can you take care of the children for a minute?

CONNECTIONS 5 – extension

Verb + Prepositions: *I don't agree with his political views.*

Write a list of verbs on one side of the board, for example:

                1. agree
                2. arrive
                3. ask

Then write a list of prepositions in jumbled order on the other side of the board, for example:

                at   with   for

Divide the class into teams of two to three players and appoint team secretaries. Then go through an example with the whole class. Pointing to the first verb on your list, say, for example: *I often have arguments with my brother. I don't agree ... his political views.* Get the class to look at the board and say what the missing preposition is from your sentence. Then begin reading sentences using the different verbs from the list, but leaving out the preposition following the verb or object. Allow time after each sentence for the team secretaries, helped by the rest of their teams, to write down the prepositions. The winner is the team with the most correct answers.

Example list of verbs and example sentences: (Adapt to the knowledge and level of your class.)

agree with	I often have arguments with my brother. I don't agree ... his political views.
arrive at	What time does this train arrive ... the station?
ask for	I hate asking my parents ... money.
believe in	Do you believe ... horoscopes?
borrow ... from	Who did you borrow that hat ...?
care about	My sister's so lazy. She doesn't care ... her examinations.
die of	The doctors couldn't say what she died ... .
divide ... into	How many pieces shall I divide the cake ...?
drive into	He's a really bad driver. He's always driving ... things.
explain to	I understand now. Thank you for explaining it ... me.
insist on	No, you paid last time. I insist ... paying now.
look at	I'm shy. Stop looking ... me.
look after	Can you look ... my children tonight? I want to go out.
prevent ... from	You can warn him, but you can't prevent him ... doing stupid things.
run into	I met an old friend yesterday. I ran ... him by chance at the bus station.
smile at	Why are you smiling ... me?
speak to	I have to speak ... you about something.
suffer from	I don't use normal soaps. I suffer ... dry skin.
take part in	He's so quiet. He never takes part ... any discussions in class.
think of/about	What are you thinking ...?
throw ... at	Don't throw any more stones ... me!
throw ... to	Throw the ball ... me.

CONNECTIONS 5

Connect the pictures with the sentences below. Then complete the sentences with the prepositions in the box.

1. [K] I think I'm going to apply ...for... this job.
2. [ ] She's apologising .... the woman .... waking her up.
3. [ ] Do these shoes belong .... you?
4. [ ] He's complaining .... the manager .... his meal.
5. [ ] I can't concentrate .... my homework.
6. [ ] What were you dreaming .... ?
7. [ ] Why are you laughing .... me?
8. [ ] I'm listening .... the neighbours.
9. [ ] I'm looking .... my socks.
10. [ ] Can you pay .... my drink?
11. [ ] Don't shout .... me!
12. [ ] Can you take care .... the children for a minute?

for		to
at		
about	on	of

© Macmillan Publishers Limited 1998.   31

MEMORY 2

Future Continuous: *You won't be sitting at your desk in the office.*

Photocopy pages 33 and 88 to play this game.

Divide the class into teams of two to three players and appoint team secretaries. Hand out page 33 and give the teams eight minutes to study and memorise the picture. Then get the teams to cover or hand you back page 33. Hand out page 88 and go through the examples with the whole class. Point out the form of the future continuous: *will + be + -ing*.

The team secretaries, helped by the rest of their team, then complete the sentences. Set a ten-minute time limit. They must not look back at the first page while doing this. The team with the most correct sentences is the winner.

> ANSWERS:
> 3. It won't be raining.
> 4. The sun will be shining.
> 5. You'll be having a delicious breakfast.
> 6. You'll be drinking fresh orange juice.
> 7. You won't be wearing a business suit.
> 8. You'll be wearing a beachrobe and sunglasses.
> 9. You won't be thinking about problems at work.
> 10. You'll be watching people swimming in the pool.
> 11. You'll be planning what beautiful places to visit.
> 12. You'll be enjoying yourself.

A GREAT DAY OUT

Future Continuous: *What will you be doing at 5 pm on Sunday?*

Write up an example diary extract on the board showing the timetable for a great day out. Base this on the local area using real names.
For example: (Adapt to the interests and age-group of your students.)

> *Sunday 25 June*
> *10–11 am get up and have a big breakfast*
> *11 am–12.30 pm drive to the seaside*
> *1–2 pm lie on the beach*
> *2–4 pm have lunch in the Seaview Café*
> *4–6 pm go on a boat trip to Smugglers' Island*
> *6–7 pm visit the Castle Museum*
> *7–9 pm have dinner in the Hilltop Restaurant*
> *10–1 am dance in Felix's Disco*

Explain that the diary extract shows what you will be doing next Sunday. Then, standing in a position where you cannot see the information on the board, get the class to ask you questions to test your memory of the events. Introduce the question: *What will you be doing at …?* Tell the students that they should ask about times in between those written on the board, i.e. ten minutes past ten but not ten o'clock. For example:

> Student: *What will you be doing at 5 pm on Sunday?*
> You: *I'll be visiting the Castle Museum.*
> Student: *What will you be doing at half past 10 in the morning?*
> You: *I'll be having breakfast.*

Get the students to plan their own timetables for a great day out on similar lines to the one on the board. Tell them to put a future date at the top of them. These timetables could be imaginary or about real plans the students have.
Divide the class into groups of two or three players. The players then swap timetables and ask questions to test each other's memories.
The winners are the players who answer all questions correctly.

MEMORY 2

Look at the picture.

You have two minutes to memorise the situation.

It's Monday morning and I'm at work. This time next week I'll be on holiday and I'm really looking forward to it.

Now look at the second page.

WORD BLUFF

Relative Pronouns (*Who/Where/Which/Whose*):
A teetotaller is someone who never drinks alcohol.
A warehouse is a place where goods are stored.
A saw is a tool which you use to cut wood or metal.
A widower is a man whose wife is dead.

Divide the class into two teams, A and B. Appoint team secretaries.
The team secretaries, helped by the rest of their team, decide which is the correct definition of the various nouns.
The first team to complete this correctly is the winner.

ANSWERS: 1b, 2c, 3a, 4b, 5c, 6c, 7a, 8b

WORD BLUFF – extension

Relative Pronouns (*Who/Where/Which/Whose*)

The team secretaries, with the help of the rest of their team, have to write eight definition puzzles similar to those on the students' page. Explain that the nouns they choose should be reasonably difficult (they may use dictionaries if they want) and should be a good mix of people, places and things so that all four relative pronouns (*who*, *where*, *which* and *whose*) are used. Check that the chosen nouns and the definitions they write are not too difficult or too easy, and that there is no duplication of nouns between the two teams.
The teams then take it in turns to read out their definition puzzles to the other team. The other team, after a few moments of group consultation, then have to choose one of the three definitions as being the correct one.
Score 1 point per correct choice.
At the end, the team with the most points is the winner.

STAR QUIZ

Relative Pronouns (*Who/Whose*): *Is it the actor who died recently?*

Write the name of a famous personality on a slip of paper, e.g. *Charlie Chaplin*. Tell the class that they have to find out the name of a famous dead actor whose name begins with the letter C. Explain that they should ask: *Is it the actor who/whose …?* questions and that they are only allowed to ask a direct question (*Is it X?*) if they get a *Yes* response from you for one of their indirect questions. For example:

Player:	*Is it the actor who died recently?*
You:	*No, it isn't.*
Player	*Is it the actor whose ex-wife sued him for a million dollars?*
You:	*No, it isn't.*
Player:	*Is it the actor who always had a little moustache?*
You:	*Yes, it is.*
Player:	*Is it Charlie Chaplin?*
You:	*Yes, it is.*

The player who guesses the right answer gets the chance to choose the name of the next famous personality for the others to guess, and so on, until everyone has had a turn. Each player should briefly introduce the personality by saying, for example:

She's a sportswoman whose name begins with the letter S; or He was a writer whose name begins with the letter H.

Word Bluff

Which is the right definition? Put a ✓ next to the correct answer.

                is someone who drinks tea.   a ☐
1. A teetotaller is someone who never drinks alcohol.   b ☐
                is someone who cannot count.   c ☐

                is a place where clothes are sold.   a ☐
2. A warehouse is a place where poor people live.   b ☐
                is a place where goods are stored.   c ☐

                is a tool which you use to cut wood or metal.   a ☐
3. A saw is a tool which you use to undo nuts.   b ☐
                is a tool which you use to pull out nails.   c ☐

                is a woman whose husband is dead.   a ☐
4. A widower is a man whose wife is dead.   b ☐
                is a child whose parents are dead.   c ☐

                is something which makes plants grow.   a ☐
5. Seasoning is something which is put on clothes to make them look pretty.   b ☐
                is something which is put on food to make it taste good.   c ☐

                are people who wear glasses.   a ☐
6. Spectators are people who watch a play or a film.   b ☐
                are people who watch an event, for example: a football match.   c ☐

                is a room where you keep food.   a ☐
7. A pantry is a room where you play games.   b ☐
                is a room where you store old unwanted things.   c ☐

                is someone who looks after cows on a farm.   a ☐
8. A coward is someone who runs away from danger.   b ☐
                is someone who helps in a hospital.   c ☐

OBSERVATION 3

Was going to: *Someone was going to shave.*

Working individually or in pairs, the players have to write five more *was going to* sentences about the picture.
The player with the most correct sentences is the winner.

> ANSWERS:
> 1. Someone was going to shave.
> 2. Someone was going to sew a button on his shirt.
> 3. Someone was going to have a meal.
> 4. Someone was going to write in the ship's log.
> 5. Someone was going to play chess.
> 6. Someone was going to mend his shoe.

INVENTION GAME

Was going to: *I was just going to do it when I noticed that I didn't have the right books.*

Explain that you are going to ask individual players why they didn't do something and that the players have to think of an excuse. For example:

> You: Why didn't you do your homework yesterday?
> Player 1: I was just going to do it when I noticed that I didn't have the right books.

The excuse must begin with *I was just going to*. Players get a minus point if they (*a*) cannot think of an adequate excuse (the excuses can be fantastic but must be something to do with the action the player is accused of not doing); or (*b*) hesitate too long.
Example round with a group of five players:

> You: Why didn't you do your homework yesterday?
> Player 1: I was just going to do it when I noticed that I didn't have the right books.
> You: Why didn't you get up yesterday?
> Player 2: I was just going to get up when I felt a terrible pain in my left leg.
> You: Why didn't you lock the door when you left the house today?
> Player 3: I was just going to lock it when I remembered that I didn't have a key to get back in again.
> You: Why didn't you sent me a postcard when you were on holiday last year?
> Player 4: (This player cannot think of an excuse and so gets a minus point.)
> You: Why didn't you send me a postcard when you were on holiday last year?
> Player 5: I was just going to send you one when I discovered that I had left my address book at home.
> You: Why didn't you phone me as you promised yesterday?
> Player 1: I was just going to phone you when they cut my phone off for not paying the bill.

And so on. The winners are the players with the least number of minus points.

Hints: Play a trial round first.
 Ask easier questions at first and then progressively make them more and more difficult.
Example accusations:

> Why didn't you come to my party last night?
> Why didn't you give your friend the message I gave you?
> Why didn't you invite me to your wedding?
> Why didn't you say hello to me yesterday when I saw you in town?
> Why didn't you tell me you had a new job?
> Why didn't you introduce me to your friend last night?
> Why didn't you give me back the book I lent you?
> Why didn't you let me know that you weren't well?

OBSERVATION 3

The story of the *Mary Celeste* is one of the greatest mysteries of the sea.

The ship was found abandoned in the Atlantic on the fourth of December 1872. It was in perfectly good order and did not seem to have been in a storm or have been attacked by pirates. The ship's log (diary) was written up to the twenty-fifth of November but again there was nothing in it to explain why the crew of eight men should suddenly leave their ship in the middle of the ocean.

Here is a picture of the cabin of the *Mary Celeste*.

Write five sentences about what the sailors were going to do just before they left the ship.

1. Someone was going to shave.
2. ......
3. ......
4. ......
5. ......
6. ......

© Macmillan Publishers Limited 1998.

PHOTOCOPIABLE

PERSONALITY QUIZ

Adjectives: *sociable*

Go through the example with the whole class. Then divide the class into teams of two to three players and get them to connect the adjectives to the people in the pictures.
The first team to do this correctly is the winner.

ANSWERS:	1. H	2. A	3. K	4. C	5. J	6. E
	7. L	8. B	9. D	10. I	11. F	12. G

WHO IS IT?

Adjectives: *She's got long, dark hair. She's kind and helpful to other people.*

Prepare a few example descriptions of famous people your students will know. They could be politicians, film stars, people in the school you work in, characters from TV soaps, sportsmen and sportswomen, etc. Use a mixture of adjectives which describe personality and adjectives which describe appearance. Read out your descriptions, for example:

She's quite young. She's got long, dark hair and is quite tall and slim. She's very sad at the moment. She's kind and helpful to other people. She's never selfish and is extremely generous.

Then get the class to ask you questions to find out who the person is. They are allowed up to 10 questions, for example:

Student:	*Is she someone in the class?*
You:	*No, she isn't.*
Student:	*Is she an singer?*
You:	*No, she isn't.*
Student:	*Is she on TV?*
You:	*Yes, she is.*
Student:	*Is she in (name of soap)?*
You:	*Yes, she is.*
Student:	*Is she (name of character)?*
You:	*Yes, she is.*

Divide the class into an even number of teams of two to three players. Get the teams to write three descriptions of famous people. Go round helping with vocabulary as they do this. Then pair up the teams and get them to take it in turns to read out their descriptions for the other team to guess.
Teams get a point for each description they guess within 10 questions. The winning teams are those with the most points.

HARRY

***So/Too* + Adjectives:** *We like Harry because he's so active. We hate Harry because he's too aggressive.*

Divide the class into two teams, Team A and Team B. Explain that Team A likes Harry whereas Team B hates him. The two teams can win points by saying why they like or hate him using *so* or *too* and adjectives beginning with each letter of the alphabet. For example, Team A, using the letter A, could say: *We like Harry because he's so active*, while Team B could say: *We hate Harry because he's too aggressive*. Score 1 point for each acceptable statement. The adjectives must be appropriate for describing why you like or hate someone. Continue in the same way with the rest of the alphabet, for example:

Team A:	*We like Harry because he's so bold.*
Team B:	*We hate Harry because he's so bossy.*
Team A:	*We like Harry because he's so clever.*
Team B:	*We hate Harry because he's so cold.*
And so on.	

At the end, the team with the highest number of points is the winner.

PERSONALITY QUIZ

Connect the adjectives describing someone's character or personality with the people.

1. sociable
2. conceited
3. generous
4. mean
5. rebellious
6. confident
7. superstitious
8. unselfish
9. vain
10. sympathetic
11. lazy
12. independent

MEMORY 3

Reflexive Pronouns/Past Continuous: *She was looking at herself in a mirror.*

Photocopy pages 41 and 89 to play this game.

Divide the class into teams of two to three players and appoint team secretaries. Hand out page 41 and give the teams two minutes to study and memorise the picture. Then get the teams to cover or hand you back page 41. Then hand out page 89 and go through the examples with the whole class. Point out that reflexive pronouns are necessary in some sentences and unnecessary in others. The team secretaries, helped by the rest of their team, then write down what the young people were doing. Set a ten-minute time limit for them to complete the sentences. They must not look back at the first page while doing this. The team with the most correct sentences is the winner.

ANSWERS:
3. She was drying herself with a towel.
4. He was relaxing under a tree.
5. He was shaving with an electric razor.
6. She was dressing behind a tree.
7. She was feeling sick.
8. He was helping himself to some sausages.

MIME GAME

Reflexive Pronouns/Present Continuous: *You're looking at yourself in the mirror.*

Write down a number of actions on slips of paper. Some of these should require a reflexive pronoun, others should not. For example: *looking at yourself in a mirror; getting dressed; washing your hands, face, body; drying yourself with a towel.*

Then hand one of the slips to a student, without any of the others in the class seeing it. Ask the student to mime the action for the others to guess, e.g. *You're looking out of a window.* (The student shakes his/her head.) *You're watching TV.* (The student shakes his/her head.) *You're looking in a mirror.* (The student indicates that the guess is close.) *You're looking at yourself in a mirror.* (The student nods.) The person who guesses the right answer gets the chance to mime the next action.

Example actions:

Cooking something.
Hurting yourself with a hammer.
Shaving.
Being annoyed with yourself.
Relaxing.
Helping yourself to some food at a party.
Trying to concentrate.
Feeling sorry for yourself.
Teaching yourself to play the guitar.
Having a guitar lesson.

MEMORY 3

Look at this picture of some young people on a camping holiday.

You have two minutes to try to memorise what everyone is doing.

Now turn to the second page.

THE WORD ORDER GAME 1

Word Order; Reflexive Pronouns; Conjunctions: *He hurt himself quite badly while skiing in Switzerland.*

Comparison of Adverbs: *You won't pass the examination unless you work harder.*

Divide the class into teams of two to three players. Appoint team secretaries.

The team secretaries, helped by the rest of their team, have to write the six sentences in the five-minute time limit.

The team with the most correct sentences is the winner.

> ANSWERS:
> 1. You won't pass the examination unless you work harder.
> 2. He lives in an ugly little house outside London.
> 3. Why do you always cut yourself while shaving?
> 4. Who speaks English the most fluently in your class?
> 5. I'm tired even though I slept well last night.
> 6. Do the English drink more tea than the French?
>   (Do the French drink more tea than the English?)

RECORDS GAME

Comparison of Adverbs: *She can see the furthest. She can see further than him.*

Divide the class into teams of three to four players.

Explain to the teams that you are going to play a number of contests to find out who can do things the best, the fastest, etc.

Announce the first contest which is to test who can see the furthest, and ask the teams to decide who is going to represent them in this contest. Only one player per team can enter.

Get the team representatives to sit at the same distance from the board. Write rows of letters, the writing becoming progressively smaller in each row as on an optician's sight-testing card. Ask the team representatives to write down as much as they can read. Ask the group to compare the individual performances, e.g. *She can see the furthest. She can see further than him.*

Continue with other contests to find out, for example:

> *Who can read the fastest.*
> *Who can draw the most realistically.*
> *Who can sing the best (or the worst!).*
> *Who can say a tongue-twister the quickest.*
> *Who can stand on one leg the longest.*
> *Who can add up the most accurately.*

THE WORD ORDER GAME 1

You have five minutes to write these sentences.

For example:

He hurt himself badly while skiing in Switzerland.

1. ....

2. ....

3. ....

4. ....

5. ....

6. ....

DIFFERENCES 1

Verbs; Vocabulary: *Don't go in there. Come here.*

Go through the example with the whole class. Then divide the class into teams of two to three players and appoint team secretaries. The team secretaries, with the help of the rest of their team, then complete the sentences with the verbs. The first team to do this correctly is the winner.

ANSWERS:	2. Bring me my coat and I'll take you home in the car. 3. Listen. Can you hear that noise? 4. Please don't lie down there. I want to lay this cloth there for the picnic. 5. Look over there. Can't you see a plane? 6. I've got to look for the baby's bottle. Can you look after her for a minute? 7. I can lend you some money for a taxi, but I'm afraid you can't borrow my car. 8. OK, you've won the last six games, but I'm going to beat you this time. 9. I hate making beds, but I love doing the laundry.

DIFFERENCES 1 – extension

Verbs; Vocabulary: look, see

Prepare a number of cards with two related verbs written on them. For example: *look – see, peep – glance, stare – watch*. Then divide the class into teams of two to three players. Shuffle and then distribute the cards amongst the teams. Ask each team to discuss their verbs and come up with two examples which clearly show the difference between the verbs. They can do this verbally or with mime. For example, a team shows the difference between *look* and *see* with the sentence: *I looked for my bag but I couldn't see it*, and then mimes peeping through a keyhole and glancing up at someone as they walk past.

Award 1 point for every clear distinction. The team with the most points at the end is the winner.

Example verbs: (Adapt to the level of your class.)

look – see
peep – glance
stare – watch
slap – punch
hit – kick
march – stroll
grin – smile
complain – grumble
drag – pull
grab – pass
pour – spill
whisper – talk
giggle – chuckle
pick up – gather
hear – listen
help – save
fall – crash
leave – go out
cook – boil
be fond of – be in love with

DIFFERENCES 1

Write the correct form of the verbs.

1. come/go

Don't ..go...... in there. ..Come.. here.

2. bring/take

.... me my coat and I'll .... you home in the car.

3. hear/listen

.... Can you .... that noise?

4. lay/lie

Please don't .... down there. I want to .... this cloth there for the picnic.

5. look/see

.... over there. Can't you .... a plane?

6. look after/look for

I've got to .... the baby's bottle. Can you .... her for a minute?

7. borrow/lend

I can .... you some money for a taxi, but I'm afraid you can't .... my car.

8. beat/win

OK, you've .... the last six games, but I'm going to .... you this time.

9. make/do

I hate .... beds, but I love .... the laundry.

© Macmillan Publishers Limited 1998.

MEMORY 4

Present Simple: *I work in a fast food restaurant in Los Angeles.*
Present Continuous: *I'm staying with a friend called Annie.*
Present Perfect Simple: *I've known Annie for two years.*
Past Simple: *I moved to Washington, DC when I was 12.*

Photocopy pages 47 and 90 to play this game.

Divide the class into teams of two to three players and appoint team secretaries. Hand out page 47 and give the teams eight minutes to study and memorise the picture. Then get the teams to cover or hand you back page 47. Hand out page 90 and go through the example with the whole class. Make it clear that they have to choose between the present simple, the present continuous, the present perfect simple and the past simple.

The team secretaries, helped by the rest of their team, then complete the sentences. Set a ten-minute time limit. They must not look back at the first page while doing this. The team with the most correct sentences is the winner.

ANSWERS:
2. I'm 25 years old.
3. My mother is a doctor.
4. I've got two sisters and a brother.
5. I moved to Washington DC when I was 12.
6. I went to high school there.
7. I then studied chemistry at the University of California.
8. I was there for two years.
9. I didn't finish my studies.
10. I work in a fast food restaurant.
11. I've been there for three weeks.
12. My last job was in a bank.
13. I worked there for six months.
14. I haven't got an apartment at the moment.
15. I'm staying with a friend called Annie.
16. I've known Annie for two years.
17. I'm taking driving lessons at the moment.
18. I've had four lessons so far.
19. I like Italian food.

MEMORY 4 – extension

Present Simple: *Do you smoke?*
Present Continuous: *Where are you living at the moment?*
Present Perfect Simple: *How long have you worked for the International Bank?*
Past Simple: *When did you move to Rome?*

Get the students to write a new identity profile for an undercover agent on similar lines to Carmen D'Souza's. Encourage them to invent new details, but stress that they should include examples of the present simple, the present continuous, the present perfect simple, and the past simple.

Divide the class into teams of two to three players. Then pair the teams and ask them to exchange their new identity profiles with a member of the other team. You should pair teams of equal size. Then give the teams time to memorise their profiles. The players then give back their profiles to the other team and then take it in turn to 'interrogate' each player on his or her new identity. For example:

Team A: *Where were you born?*
Player B: *In Paris.*
Team A: *When did you move to Rome?*
Player B: *Three years ago.*
Team A: *Where are you living at the moment?*
Player B: *In the Hilton Hotel in London.*
Team A: *How long have you worked for the International Bank?*
Player B: *Two years.*
Team A: *Do you smoke?*
Player B: *Yes, I do.*

If a player makes a mistake, his or her cover is blown and the team go on to question the next agent. The winners are the players who do not blow their cover and answer all questions correctly. The winning teams are those with the most agents who answer all their questions correctly.

MEMORY 4

CARMEN D'SOUZA IS A POLICE AGENT. I WANT HER TO DO SOME UNDERCOVER WORK. SHE HAS TO PRETEND TO BE SOMEONE ELSE. THIS IS HER NEW IDENTITY. PRETEND YOU ARE CARMEN. YOU HAVE EIGHT MINUTES TO MEMORISE IT.

 1. You were born in Sydney, Australia.

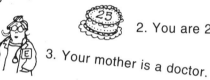 2. You are 25 years old.

3. Your mother is a doctor.

 4. You've got two sisters and a brother.

5. You moved to Washington, DC when you were 12.

 6. You went to high school there.

7. You then studied chemistry at the University of California.

 8. You were there for two years.

9. You didn't finish your studies.

10. You work in a fast food restaurant in Los Angeles.

 11. You've been there for three weeks.

12. Your last job was in a bank.

13. You worked there for six months.

 14. You haven't got an apartment at the moment.

 15. You're staying with a friend called Annie.

16. You've known Annie for two years.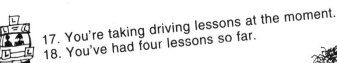

17. You're taking driving lessons at the moment.

18. You've had four lessons so far.

19. You like Italian food.

NOW LOOK AT THE SECOND PAGE.

© Macmillan Publishers Limited 1998.

PHOTOCOPIABLE

CONNECTIONS 6

Adjectives + Prepositions: *I'm afraid of spiders*

Go through the example with the whole class. Then get the players, working individually or in teams of two to three, to match the pictures with the sentences. They should then complete the sentences with the correct form of the prepositions. Set an eight-minute time limit to complete the game. The player/team with the most correct sentences is the winner.

ANSWERS:	
2. J I'm amazed at the size of the dog.	7. A Are you engaged to him?
3. H I'm very angry with you.	8. K He's famous for his ice cream.
4. E I'm really bad at drawing.	9. G I'm very interested in cookery.
5. C I'm bored with this book.	10. I It was very nice of you to give me a present.
6. L She's very different from her brother.	11. B Stop being rude to your father.
	12. F I'm worried about tomorrow's examination.

CONNECTIONS 6 – extension

Adjectives + Prepositions: *She gets very anxious about being near a dog.*

Write a list of adjectives on one side of the board, for example:

       1. anxious
       2. astonished
       3. clever
       (etc., see list below)

Then write a list of prepositions in jumbled order on the other side of the board, for example:

       at   by   about
       (etc., see list below)

Divide the class into teams of two to three players and appoint team secretaries. Then go through an example with the whole class. Pointing to the first adjective on your list, say, for example: *My sister hates dogs. She gets very anxious ... being near a dog.* Get the class to look at the board and say what the missing preposition is from your sentence. Then begin reading sentences using the different adjectives from the list, but leaving out the preposition following the adjective. Allow time after each sentence for the team secretaries, helped by the rest of their teams, to write down the prepositions.
The winner is the team with the most correct answers.
Example list of verbs and example sentences: (Adapt to the knowledge and level of your class.)

anxious about	My sister hates dogs. She gets very anxious ... being near a dog.
astonished at/by	I'm always astonished ... how few people speak English.
clever at	That's right. You're very clever ... guessing things.
disappointed with	I'd hoped I'd do well in the exam. But I was very disappointed ... my mark.
disgusted with/by	He's horrible to me. I'm disgusted ... his behaviour.
good at	Are you any good ... mending things?
ill with	He can't come to school. He's ill ... food poisoning.
impressed with/by	She's very young, but I was impressed ... how well she played.
kind to	I like him very much. He's always so kind ... me.
pleased with	Were you pleased ... your presents?
polite to	Always be polite ... your grandparents.
red with	He was red ... anger.
responsible for	Who is responsible ... this mistake?
shocked at/by	I was shocked ... the bad language used in the film.
wrong with	You're so bad-tempered. What's wrong ... you?

CONNECTIONS 6

Connect the pictures with the sentences below. Then complete the sentences with the prepositions in the box.

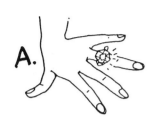
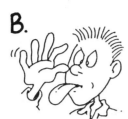

1. [D] I'm afraid *of* .... spiders.
2. [ ] I'm amazed .... the size of the dog.
3. [ ] I'm very angry .... you.
4. [ ] I'm really bad .... drawing.
5. [ ] I'm bored .... this book.
6. [ ] She's very different .... her brother.
7. [ ] Are you engaged .... him?
8. [ ] He's famous .... his ice cream.
9. [ ] I'm very interested .... cookery.
10. [ ] It was very nice .... you to give me a present.
11. [ ] Stop being rude .... your father.
12. [ ] I'm worried .... tomorrow's examination.

from		to
	about	
with	of	at
in		for

© Macmillan Publishers Limited 1998.

MEMORY 5

Past Perfect Continuous: *Because she had been swimming.*

Photocopy pages 51 and 91 to play this game.

Divide the class into teams of two to three players and appoint team secretaries. Hand out page 51 and give the teams two minutes to study and memorise the picture. Then get the teams to cover or hand you back page 51. Hand out page 91 and go through the example with the whole class. Point out the form of the past perfect continuous: *had + been + -ing* form.

The team secretaries, helped by the rest of their team, then write down the answers to the questions. Set a ten-minute time limit for them to complete the sentences. They must not look back at the first page while doing this. The team with the most correct sentences is the winner.

> ANSWERS:
> 2. Because he had been helping her.
> 3. Because she had been shopping.
> 4. Because they had been jogging.
> 5. Because he had been writing graffiti on the wall.
> 6. Because he had been mending his motorbike.
> 7. Because they had been waiting for a bus for over half an hour.
> 8. Because they had been travelling all day.
> 9. Because a woman had been cleaning her car.

LONG SENTENCE GAME

Past Perfect Continuous: *She'd been typing letters all day.*

Begin the game by saying to the nearest student to you, for example, *Gloria works in an office. She was very tired when she finished work last night. She'd been typing letters all day.* Explain that this player has to repeat what you have said to the next player and then add another action that Gloria had been doing in the office, for example, *She'd been making telephone calls.* The game continues with each player in turn trying to remember what the last players said and then adding something new to the list. Players get a minus point if they (*a*) make a memory mistake; (*b*) say an action inappropriate to the situation of someone working in an office; (*c*) hesitate too long. Do not give players minus points for grammar mistakes – just correct the mistake and let the next player continue. Example round:

Player 1: *She'd been typing letters all day.*
Player 2: *She'd been typing letters all day. She'd been making telephone calls.*
Player 3: *She'd been typing letters all day. She'd been making telephone calls. She'd been filing documents.*
Player 4: *She'd been typing letters all day. She'd been ...*
(This player hesitates too long and so gets a minus point.)
Player 5: (continues) *She'd been typing letters all day. She'd been making telephone calls. She'd been filing documents. She'd been writing reports.*
Player 6: *She'd been typing letters all day. She'd been making telephone calls. She'd been filing letters.* (This player makes a memory mistake and so gets a minus point.)
And so on.

At the end, the player with the least number of minus points is the winner.
Hints: Play a trial round before playing for real.

Look at these people.

You have two minutes to try to memorise the situation.

NOW ANSWER THE QUESTIONS ON THE SECOND PAGE.

SPOT THE DIFFERENCE 3

Passive – *Has been done*: *The front door has been mended.*
Curtains have been put up.

Divide the class into teams of two to three players. Appoint team secretaries.
The team secretaries, helped by the rest of their team, try to find six more differences between picture A and picture B. Set a five-minute time limit.
The team with the most correct sentences is the winner.

| ANSWERS: | The bathroom has been modernised.
The fence has been repaired.
Central heating has been put in.
The grass has been cut.
The front door has been painted.
The roof has been retiled. |
|---|---|

WHAT'S DIFFERENT?

Passive – *Has been done*: *The board has been cleaned.*

Ask a player to come to the front of the room and look carefully around the room. Then ask this player to leave the room for a moment.
While the player is out of the room, with the help of the class make five changes to objects in the room, e.g. *clean the board, empty the bin, open a window, close the lid of the tape-recorder, switch on the light.*
The player then comes back in and tries to find out what has been changed. For example:

> *The board has been cleaned.*
> *The bin has been emptied.*
> *The window has been opened.*

Score 1 point for each correct observation.
Then ask another player to leave the room for a moment while the class make five more changes to objects in the room. And so on, until every player has had a turn.
At the end, the player with the most points is the winner.
Hints: With a large class you could speed this game up by playing it with pair teams.

Spot the Difference 3

Compare these two pictures. Picture A shows a house in very bad condition, picture B shows the same house a few months later. Write what has been done to the house.

Use these words:					
the front door	the bathroom	the fence	the roof	central heating	the grass
paint	modernise	put in	retile	cut	repair

The front door has been mended.

Curtains have been put up.

Find six more differences in picture B.

1. ....
2. ....
3. ....
4. ....
5. ....
6. ....

© Macmillan Publishers Limited 1998.

MEMORY 6

Past Perfect: *You had just got on the bus.*
Past Continuous: *You were just getting on the bus.*
Was going to: *You were just going to get on the bus.*

Photocopy pages 55 and 92 to play this game.

The class can either work individually or in pairs. Hand out page 55 and give them two minutes to study and memorise the picture. Then get them to cover or hand you back page 55. Hand out page 92. The players write what happened in the accident using the sentences on page 92. They must not look back at the first page while doing this. The player with the most correct answers is the winner.

> ANSWERS:
> 1. You were just getting on the bus.
> 2. A car was just overtaking the bus.
> 3. A cyclist had just overtaken the bus.
> 4. An old lady was just crossing the road.
> 5. A man had just parked his car.
> 6. Two children were just going to cross the road.
> 7. A woman was just going to get out of the car.
> 8. A van was just turning left.

MEMORY 6 – extension

Past Perfect: *You had just stood up.*
Past Continuous: *You were reading a book.*
Was going to: *You were just going to do some work.*

Ask all the players to do something, e.g. *read a book, write something, look out of the window, look for something in their bags, take something out of their pocket, stand up, tidy up possessions, get ready to leave, prepare to do some work, speak to someone.*

Then ask a player to stand in front of the class and look carefully at everyone in the room and what they are doing. Ask this player to leave the room for a moment.

When the player has left the room, ask everybody to remember exactly what they *had just done, were doing* or *were just going to do* when the player was looking at them. They should stop doing these actions at this stage.

The player then comes back in and tries to remember what everybody was doing when he or she left the room. For example:

> *You had just stood up.*
> *You were reading a book.*
> *You were just going to do some work.*

Score 1 point for each correct observation.
Continue with each player in turn. Get everybody to try to think of new, interesting things to do for each round.
At the end, the player with the most points is the winner.

Accident ...
You were waiting at the bus-stop when you saw this accident. The police are going to ask you to say what you saw.

Look at the picture for two minutes.

Try to remember everything that happened.

THE WORD ORDER GAME 2

Word Order; Adverbs of Frequency: *Have you ever been to New York?*

Divide the class into teams of two to three players. Appoint team secretaries.
The team secretaries, helped by the rest of their team, have to write the six sentences in the four-minute time limit.
The team with the most correct sentences is the winner.

ANSWERS:	2. I never go to the library on Saturday. (On Saturday I never go to the library.)
	3. How much money do you usually give them?
	4. This is the most interesting book I have ever read.
	5. Does he always cook so well?
	6. She often catches the eight o'clock bus to work.
	7. Did you ever steal apples when you were a boy? (a child)

THE WORD ORDER GAME 2 – extension

Word Order

Ask each team to think of a sentence between ten and fourteen words long. The sentence could be a question or an affirmative or negative statement. The team secretaries should then write out the sentences, putting each word on a separate piece of paper. Remind them to write the question mark on a separate piece of paper if they have chosen to write a question.

Check all the sentences to see that they are correct and that each word has been written out on a separate piece of paper. Encourage the teams to make the sentences quite complex with the use of clauses and parts of speech like adverbs of frequency (*often*, *always*, *seldom*, etc.), adverbs of manner (*quickly*, *badly*, *well*, etc.), and adjectives.

Each team then hands their sentences – in jumbled order – to the next team who try to rearrange it into a proper sentence.

Time how long it takes for each team to do this (you may have to appoint a player as an additional timekeeper to help you) and award points in terms of how many seconds it takes. For example:

Team A – 35.

The teams then pass on the sentence – again in jumbled order – to the next team, and so on, until the teams have worked on all the sentences.
At the end, the team with the **lowest** total of points is the winner.

THE WORD ORDER GAME 2

You have four minutes to write the sentences.

1. Have you ever been to New York?

2. ....

3. ....

4. ....

5. ....

6. ....

7. ....

MEMORY 7

Reported Speech: *The announcement said all passengers to Lagos should go immediately to Gate Five.*

Photocopy pages 59 and 93 to play this game.

Divide the class into teams of two to three players. Appoint team secretaries. Hand out page 59. The team secretaries, helped by the rest of their team, write the letters A–M in the correct speech balloons. Then get the teams to cover or hand you back page 59. Hand out page 93. They then look at this second page and write down what the various people at the airport said, using the prompts. They must not look back at the first page while doing this.
The team with the most correct sentences is the winner.

ANSWERS:
A. The announcement said all passengers to Lagos should go immediately to Gate Five.
B. The stewardess said they could wait by the check-in counter.
C. The passenger said he came from Australia.
D. The young man reminded her not to forget to write.
E. The man with the beard said he hadn't got anything in his bag.
F. The security officer told him to walk through the door.
G. The wife said they ought to hurry.
H. The girl explained that she had had an accident.
I. The mother said the plane was going to land.
J. The man with the rucksack told him he was staying for two weeks.
K. The young man said he had just arrived at the airport.
L. The old man said he had been very afraid.
M. The husband said he would fetch a trolley.

BUSH-TELEGRAPH

Reported Speech: *You said you didn't feel very well.*

Begin by saying *I don't feel very well*. Explain that the first player has to report what you said and then say something new for the next player to remember and report, e.g. *You said you didn't feel very well. I feel fine*. The game continues in this way with each player in turn trying to remember what the other players said and then saying something new.
Players get a minus point if they (*a*) make a memory mistake; or (*b*) hesitate too long.
Example round with a group of five players:

Player 1: *You said you didn't feel very well. I feel fine.*
Player 2: *You said you didn't feel very well. You said you felt fine. I felt fine until a moment ago.*
Player 3: *You said you didn't feel very well. You said you felt fine. You said you had felt fine until a moment ago. I'm going out.*
Player 4: *You said ...*
 (This player cannot remember what follows and gets a minus point.)
Player 5: (beginning again) *I'm very happy.*
Player 1: *You said you were very happy. I'll be glad when this lesson is over.*

And so on.

At the end, the players with the least number of minus points are the winners.
Hints: Play a trial round first.

CLOSE UPS

Have something done: *He's having his hair dyed.*

Go through the example with the whole class. Point out the passive form *have* + object + past participle. Then divide the class into teams of two to three players and appoint team secretaries. The team secretaries, helped by the rest of their team, then write sentences about each picture using the verbs in the box. The winner is the first team to do this correctly.

> ANSWERS:
> 2. He's having his back massaged.
> 3. He's having his toenails cut.
> 4. He's having his beard trimmed.
> 5. He's having his eyes tested.
> 6. He's having his shirt pressed.
> 7. He's having his shoes polished.
> 8. He's having his socks mended.
> 9. He's having his suit dry cleaned.
> 10. He's having his photograph taken.

INVENTION GAME

Have something done (or **Get something done**): *I need to have the brakes adjusted.*

Prepare some descriptions about different things using the structure *have* (or *get*) + object + past participle. For example:

There are lots of things wrong with it. I need to have the brakes adjusted. I also need to have the clutch repaired and a new windscreen wiper fitted.

Explain that you are going to read out some descriptions and that the teams have to guess what object you are talking about. Read out the first description as an example:

There are lots of things wrong with it. I need to have the brakes adjusted. I also need to have the clutch repaired and a new windscreen wiper fitted. What am I talking about?

Get the class to guess that you are talking about your car.
Divide the class into teams of two to three players and appoint team secretaries. The team secretaries, helped by the rest of their team, have to write down the name of the object you are talking about. Begin to read out your descriptions stopping after each one for the teams to discuss and write down their answer. The winning team is the one that guesses the most objects.
Example descriptions: (Adapt to the level of your class.)

There are lots of things wrong with it. I need to have the brakes adjusted. I also need to have the clutch repaired and a new windscreen wiper fitted. (a car)

I had it dyed black. It was a really horrible colour before. I also had some new buttons put on and the sleeves shortened. (a coat, cardigan, or jacket)

I should have the roof repaired. I also need to have the plumbing ripped out and completely replaced and then I must have the whole place repainted. (a house)

You should have the front tyre repaired. Two spokes in the back wheel are broken so you should have those replaced. Also, you should have the saddle raised. It's too low for you at the moment. (a bicycle)

You could have it permed, I suppose. Or you could have it cut short. That might look nice. (hair)

I'm having it developed at the moment. Then I'm going to have them all enlarged and framed. (a film, photographs)

I had two extracted and three filled. Then I had them all cleaned and polished. Don't they look nice? (teeth)

CLOSE-UPS

What is this man having done?

Use these verbs: press, cut, mend, massage, test, take, dry clean, trim, polish, dye

1. He's having his hair dyed.
2. ....
3. ....
4. ....
5. ....
6. ....
7. ....
8. ....
9. ....
10. ....

OBSERVATION 4

Passive – *Had been done*: *Rock'n'roll hadn't been thought of yet.*

Divide the class into teams of two to three players. Appoint team secretaries.
The team secretaries, helped by the rest of their team, write down five more sentences pointing out the deliberate mistakes in the picture.
The first team to do this correctly is the winner.

ANSWERS:	The atomic bomb hadn't been invented yet. (1945)
	The Sound of Music hadn't been made yet. (1965)
	Penicillin hadn't been developed yet. (1940)
	Guernica hadn't been painted yet. (by Pablo Picasso 1937)
	Mohammed Ali (Cassius Clay) hadn't been born yet. (1950)

OBSERVATION 4 – extension

Passive – *Had been done*: *The Arc de Triomphe hadn't been built yet.*

You will need a number of stories with a historical setting for this game.
Tell the class that you are going to tell them a story about Napoleon which contains a number of deliberate mistakes. The players should listen to the story and interrupt you whenever they spot a mistake.
Begin to read the story:

> *It was the year 1811. Napoleon looked out of the windows of his state room which overlooked all Paris. In front of him he could see the Arc de Triomphe reminding him of all his great victories. On the horizon was the Eiffel Tower. 'Why didn't Eiffel call it the Napoleon Tower?', thought Napoleon. He picked up a gold telescope lying on the table next to him. 'Perhaps I can see Josephine,' he murmured. 'No, she must have gone to see one of those new-fangled Lumière brothers' cinematographs,' he thought as he scanned the palace for signs of Josephine. He looked at the picture of George Washington on the wall. 'Did he have the same problems as me?' he wondered. He picked up a book and switched on his desk light. It was 'War and Peace'. Napoleon loved to read books which were about war. 'If only it was called "War and War",' he thought. 'Now that would be a book' The telephone rang. 'Ah, well. Back to business! I suppose that's Marshal Ney with the latest news about the Battle of Waterloo,' he speculated.*

And so on, with the players coming in with interruptions such as:

> *The Arc de Triomphe hadn't been built yet.*
> *Eiffel hadn't been born yet.*
> *The cinematograph hadn't been invented yet.*

(Other deliberate mistakes: *electric light/invented, War and Peace/written, telephone/invented, Battle of Waterloo/fought.*)

Hints: You could get teams of players to write similar stories to test the rest of the group's historical knowledge.

OBSERVATION 4

This scene shows the notorious American gangster Al Capone with his gang in a Chigago nightclub in 1929. There are a number of deliberate mistakes in the picture.

Rock 'n' roll hadn't been thought of yet.

Find five more deliberate mistakes.

| Use these verbs: | invent | make | develop | paint | born |

1. ....

2. ....

3. ....

4. ....

5. ....

CONNECTIONS 7

Phrasal Verbs: *Who is Danny going out with?*

Go through the example with the whole class. Then, working individually or in teams of two to three, the players match the pictures with the phrasal verbs in the box. They should then complete the questions with the correct form of the phrasal verbs. Set an eight-minute time limit to complete the game. The player/team with the most correct sentences is the winner.

ANSWERS:	2. What time did the plane take off?
	3. Why have you put off your dental appointment?
	4. What time are you going to wake up tomorrow morning?
	5. Have you filled in the form?
	6. Why has Julia fallen out with Danny?
	7. Why did your car break down?
	8. Are you going to tell off the children?
	9. Do you take after your father or your mother?
	10. When did your grandfather pass away?
	11. Can you look after my children for half an hour?
	12. Can I see you off at the station?

DRAWING GAME

Phrasal Verbs: *throw away, look forward to, grow up*

Draw up a list of phrasal verbs appropriate to the level of your students. Ideally, these phrasal verbs should be taken from teaching materials (texts, dialogues, etc.) used in past lessons with your students. As an example, write up a list of five of these phrasal verbs on the board. Number these verbs 1–5. Then draw – in jumbled order – simple blackboard drawings representing these verbs alongside them. Label these drawings A–E. Then ask the class, working in teams of two or three, to match your drawings with the verbs in the list. For example:

1. run over

2. grow up

3. throw away

4. give up

5. look forward to

Then give a list of five different phrasal verbs to each team. Get the teams to copy this list on a separate piece of paper and draw a picture in jumbled order representing each verb in their list as you did in the example. Go round the class helping with comprehension and ideas as they do this.
Then get the teams to exchange papers and match the drawings with the phrasal verbs. Teams win 1 point for each verb they guess.

CONNECTIONS 7

Match the phrasal verbs with the pictures. Then complete the questions with the correct form of the verb.

| fall out | go out with | look after | pass away | see off | take after | tell off |
| fill in | | | break down | put off | | take off | wake up |

1. Who is Danny .... *going out with* ....? – Julia.

2. What time did the plane ....? – At 12.30.

3. Why have you .... your dental appointment tomorrow? – Because I'm too busy.

4. What time are you going to .... tomorrow morning? – At 7.00.

5. Have you .... the form? – Yes, I have.

6. Why has Julia .... with Danny? – Because he was rude to her.

7. Why did your car ....? – It ran out of petrol.

8. Are you going to .... the children? – Yes.

9. Do you .... your father or your mother? – My father.

10. When did your grandfather ....? – Last year.

11. Can you .... my children for half an hour? – Of course.

12. Can I .... you .... at the station? – No, let's say goodbye here.

TRUE OR FALSE?   Comprehension

Working individually or in pairs, the players read the three possible explanations and decide which is the true one.

> ANSWER: The true story is C.

TRUE OR FALSE – extension   Comprehension

You could extend this game by making up or finding interesting derivations of words and then reading them to the players who have to decide whether the explanation is true or false. For example:

The word 'news' comes from the initial letters of the words 'north', 'east', 'west', 'south'. This is because it is the latest information coming in from the four points of the compass.

(False: It comes from the old French word 'noveles'.)

The expression 'OK' comes from the initials of a Mr Otto Keiser who worked for the Ford Motor Company in the USA in the early part of this century. Mr Keiser worked as chief checker for Ford and his job consisted of standing at the end of the assembly line checking that the newly finished cars were road-worthy. Mr Keiser had the habit of chalking his initials on the cars that passed his tests. And in time these initials 'OK' have come to mean OK.

(False: There are many theories for the derivation of 'OK' but this is certainly not one of them.)

Cardigans are named after the British nobleman, the Earl of Cardigan who began the fashion for wearing this garment in his efforts to try to keep warm while fighting in the Crimean War.

(True)

The players, working individually or in pairs, and with the aid of dictionaries, could then write similar true and false derivations for the rest of the class to guess.

True or False?

Why is a sandwich called a sandwich?
Only one of these stories is true. Which is it?

Put a ✓ in the box next to the true story.

English people love picnics. They like eating in the countryside, in parks and even on the beach. The only problem about eating on the beach is that the sand often gets into the food. One day someone had the very good idea of putting the meat or cheese between two slices of bread. This stopped the sand from getting onto the food. It is because of this that today we call sandwiches 'sandwiches'.

A. ☐

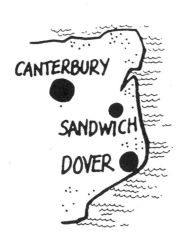

The town of Sandwich is situated between Dover and Canterbury in south-east England. Sandwich is a very small town when you compare it with either Dover or Canterbury but the people who live there have always considered that it is a more important and better town to live in than either of the other two larger towns. One day a Sandwich man was sitting having lunch with a man from Dover and a man from Canterbury. The Sandwich man put a thick slice of bread on the table and said, 'This piece of bread is Canterbury'. Then he put another thick slice of bread on top of the first slice and said, 'And this is Dover'. Then he picked up a piece of cheese, put it between the two slices of bread and said, 'But this tasty piece of cheese is Sandwich'. It is because of this man that today we call sandwiches 'sandwiches'.

B. ☐

An eighteenth-century English aristocrat, the Earl of Sandwich, loved playing cards. He used to play cards all day and night and hated having to stop a game for his meals. One day he thought of a way of putting meat between two slices of bread. In this way he could eat while at the same time continue playing cards. It is because of the Earl of Sandwich that today we call sandwiches 'sandwiches'.

C. ☐

© Macmillan Publishers Limited 1998.

DIFFERENCES 2

American and British English; Vocabulary:
car, automobile

Go through the example with the whole class. Then divide the class into teams of two to three players and appoint team secretaries. The team secretaries, with the help of the rest of their team, first write the American English expressions under the correct pictures and then match these expressions with their British English equivalent. The first team to do this correctly is the winner.

ANSWERS:		
	1. apartment – E	10. garbage can – K
	2. automobile – A	11. movie – J
	3. can – P	12. pants – G
	4. candy – M	13. panty-hose – B
	5. cookie – F	14. purse – C
	6. diaper – I	15. rest room – H
	7. elevator – D	16. shorts – O
	8. eraser – R	17. truck – N
	9. expressway – Q	18. sidewalk – L

WHAT ARE THEY TALKING ABOUT?

American and British English; Vocabulary:
faucet, tap

Divide the class into teams of two to three players and appoint team secretaries. Explain that you are going to read out some sentences containing two American English expressions which have different British English equivalents and that the teams have to guess what is being talked about and try to write down the British English equivalents. Work through one or two examples with the whole class.

Then begin to read out the sentences getting the team secretaries, helped by the rest of their team, to write down their ideas. Give the teams time to discuss and write down their answers before going on to the next sentence.

Award 1 point for each correct British English equivalent. The winning team is the one with the most points at the end.

Example sentences:

One of the faucets won't work on the tub.
(One of the taps won't work on the bath.)
First the fender fell off and then I couldn't open the trunk.
(First the bumper fell off (the car) and then I couldn't open the boot.)
Go over the overpass and turn left at the intersection.
(Go over the flyover and turn left at the crossroads.)
I have to buy a crib and baby-carriage.
(I've got to buy a cot and pram.)
The closet is full of trash.
(The cupboard is full of rubbish.)
Where did you buy those sneakers? What was the name of the store?
(Where did you buy those trainers. What was the name of the shop?)
I'm mad because you're stingy.
(I'm angry because you're mean.)
The subway's someplace near here.
(The tube/underground is somewhere near here.)
Do you want one-way or a round-trip?
(Do you want a single (ticket) or a return?)
Don't peek at me while I'm in the rest room.
(Don't peep at me while I'm in the toilet.)
My billfold is in my pocket book.
(My wallet is in my handbag.)
Did you mail the package?
(Did you post the parcel?)
I bought this topcoat last fall.
(I bought this overcoat last autumn.)

DIFFERENCES 2

Write these American English expressions under the pictures.

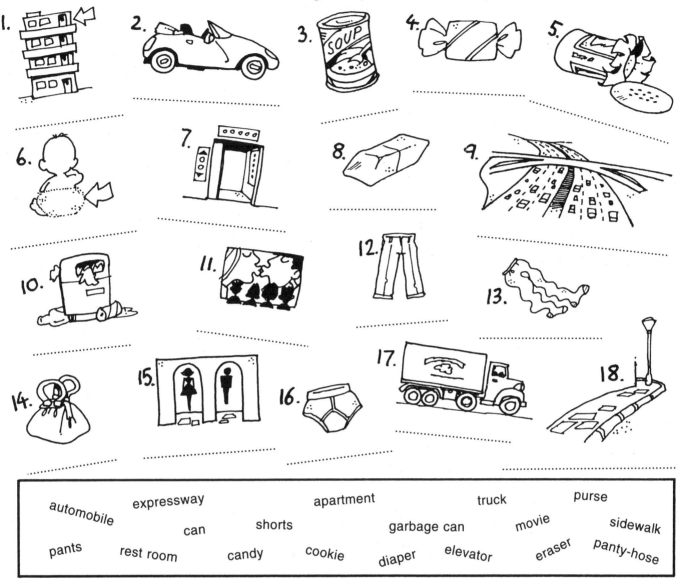

automobile	expressway	apartment	truck	purse
pants	can	shorts	garbage can	movie	sidewalk
	rest room	candy	cookie	diaper	elevator	eraser	panty-hose

Now connect the American expressions with their British English equivalents.

A. car *automobile*

B. tights ....

C. handbag ....

D. lift ....

E. flat ....

F. biscuit ....

G. trousers ....

H. public toilet ....

I. nappy ....

J. film ....

K. rubbish bin ....

L. pavement ....

M. sweet ....

N. lorry ....

O. pants ....

P. tin ....

Q. motorway ....

R. rubber ....

© Macmillan Publishers Limited 1998.

OBSERVATION 5

Should have done: *He should have cleaned his rifle.*

Working individually or in pairs, the players have to write eight more sentences about what George should have done. Set a five-minute time limit. The player with the most correct sentences wins.

ANSWERS:	He should have shaved.	He should have emptied the ashtray.
	He should have polished his boots.	He should have hung up his clothes.
	He should have made his bed.	He should have sewn on the button.
	He should have taken down the photographs.	He should have combed his hair

LONG SENTENCES GAME

Shouldn't have done: *You shouldn't have drunk so much.*

Begin the game by saying *You shouldn't have drunk so much*. Explain that the first player has to repeat this sentence and add a new criticism to accuse the next player of, e.g. *You shouldn't have drunk so much and broken that window*. The game continues with each player in turn trying to remember what the last player said, and then adding a new item to the sentence.

Players get a minus point if they (*a*) make a memory mistake; or (*b*) hesitate too long. Do not penalise players for grammar mistakes – just correct the mistake and let the player continue.

Example round with a group of five players:

Player 1: *You shouldn't have drunk so much and broken that window.*
Player 2: *You shouldn't have drunk so much, broken that window, and shouted so much.*
Player 3: *You shouldn't have drunk so much, broken that window, shouted so much and danced with the policeman.*
Player 4: *You shouldn't have drunk so much, shouted so much …*
(*This player makes a memory mistake and so gets a minus point.*)
Player 5: (beginning again) *You shouldn't have made so much fuss.*
Player 1: *You shouldn't have made so much fuss and become so angry.*

And so on. The player with the least number of minus points is the winner.

Hints: Play a trial round first. You could play further rounds with different starters, for example:
You should have asked more questions.
You should have asked more questions and worked harder.

INVENTION GAME

Should have done: *You should have driven more slowly.*
Shouldn't have done: *You shouldn't have overtaken the lorry.*

Divide the class into teams of two to three players. Appoint team secretaries.
Write up *I had an accident in my car*. Explain that the team secretaries, helped by the rest of their team, have to write down as many appropriate criticisms with *you should have* and *you shouldn't have* as they can think of. For example: *You should have driven more slowly. You shouldn't have overtaken the lorry.* Tell the teams that they shouldn't write sentences which simply say the same thing in a different way, e.g. *You should have driven more slowly. You shouldn't have driven so fast.*
Set a three-minute time limit. Then get each team to read out their list in turn. As the other teams read out their sentences, the team secretaries should cross out any duplicate sentences on their own list. At the end, the team with the most original sentences left is the winner. (Check that all the remaining sentences are correct and that they are appropriate to the situation of a road accident.)

Hints: You could play further rounds with new situations, for example:

I was sacked from my job.   *I didn't pass the exam.*
Burglars broke into my house.   *We lost the tennis match.*
My wife/husband left me.   *My business has gone bankrupt.*
I didn't get the job.   *This food I've just cooked tastes terrible.*

OBSERVATION 5

George is not a very good soldier. He always gets told off when the sergeant inspects his room every Monday morning. It is Monday now and the sergeant is soon going to make his inspection. What should George have done?

He should have cleaned his rifle.

Write eight more sentences about what George should have done before the inspection this morning.

Use these verbs: shave, hang up, polish, make, sew on, take down, comb, empty

1. ....
2. ....
3. ....
4. ....
5. ....
6. ....
7. ....
8. ....

© Macmillan Publishers Limited 1998.

PHOTOCOPIABLE

DETECTIVE

Must have done: *He must have hidden in the cupboard or in the chest.*

Divide the class into teams of two to three players. Appoint team secretaries.
The team secretaries, helped by the rest of their team, write answers to the questions about the robbery. Set a three-minute time limit. The team with the most correct answers is the winner.

> ANSWERS:
> 1. He must have hidden in the cupboard or in the chest.
> 2. He must have used the candle or the lamp.
> 3. He must have stood on the desk or the stool.
> 4. He must have used the sword or the dagger.
> 5. He must have got out of the window or the fanlight.

DEDUCTION GAME

Could have done: *The cats could have had very poor eyesight.*
Could have been doing: *The man could have been smoking.*

You need a number of puzzle situations for this game.
Divide the class into two teams and appoint team secretaries.
Explain that you are going to read out a situation which could be explained in a number of ways:

> *There was a pipe, 150 cm long and 30 cm wide. A cat walked to one end of the pipe and looked in. Another cat walked to the other end of the pipe and looked in. They didn't see each other. What could be the explanation?*

Then discuss possible explanations, for example:

> *The cats could have had very poor eyesight.*
> *It could have been very dark.*
> *The pipe could have been bent.*
> *There could have been something in the middle of the pipe.*
> *The cats could have both blinked at the same moment.*

If nobody suggests it, tell them the 'true' explanation: *The cats looked in the pipe at different times.*

Read out another situation:

> *A car was being driven with no headlights. In front of the car a man was crossing the road. He was dressed completely in black. His back was turned so the driver couldn't see his face. There were no street lights yet the driver managed to brake and stop in time. What could be the explanation?*

The team secretaries, helped by the rest of their team, then have to write down as many possible explanations as they can think of. The explanations can be imaginative, even fantastic, but they must be logically possible. For example:

> *The man could have lit a cigarette.*
> *The man could have been smoking.*
> *The driver could have had very good night vision.*
> *There could have been a full moon.*
> *The driver could have wanted to stop anyway.*
> *The driver could have stopped by intuition.*
> *The man could have been singing very loudly.*

The two teams then read out their explanations. The team secretaries should cross out any duplicate explanations read out by the other team. At the end, the team with the most sentences left is the winner. Get the two teams to check that the other team's explanations are logically possible. Again, if nobody thought of it tell them the 'true' explanation: *It happened in the middle of the day.*

DETECTIVE

A very valuable painting was stolen from this museum last night. The police think the robbery happened something like this ...

A 'visitor' stayed behind when the museum closed at five.

The thief hid somewhere while the security guard checked the room.

He then came out after the guards had left, cut the alarm wire and stole the painting.

He must have used objects in the room in the museum to carry out the robbery as all visitors are searched when they enter the museum.

1. He must have hidden in the cupboard or in the chest.

Write two possibilities for each question.

2. ....
3. ....
4. ....
5. ....

CATEGORIES 2

Verb + -ing: *I enjoy staying in bed.*
Verb + to Infinitive: *I refuse to move.*

Go through the examples with the whole class. Then, working individually or in teams of two to three players, the players write sentences for each picture under the correct column and using *-ing* or the *to* infinitive. The first player/team to complete this correctly is the winner.

ANSWERS:	*-ing* form	*to* infinitive
	I enjoy staying in bed.	I refuse to move.
	I feel like going for a swim.	I can't afford to stay here.
	I can't help snoring.	I expect to find a job soon.
	I avoid going on the roads.	I promise to write to you.
	I keep on making the same mistake.	I hope to get out without him seeing me.
	I miss going to work	I want to see that film.

INVENTION GAME

Verb + -ing: *The thief admitted taking the CD player.*
Verb + to Infinitive: *What time did you arrange to come?*

Prepare a list of prompts which will elicit verb + *-ing* and verb + *to* infinitive combinations, for example:

The thief admitted ... ; What time did you arrange ...; My parents gave up ...; etc.

Write the list of verbs on the board, for example:

admit   arrange   give up

Then work through a few examples with the whole class. For example, point to the first verb on your list, *admit*, say: *The thief admitted ...* and elicit from the class some possible ways of ending this sentence:

The thief admitted taking the CD player. The thief admitted stealing the money. The thief admitted breaking into the house.

Divide the class into teams of two to three players and appoint team secretaries. Explain that the teams have to think of ways of ending the sentences you read out with either the *-ing* form or the *to* infinitive. Read out the prompts. Set a time limit of two minutes after each one for the teams to discuss and for the team secretaries to write down their answers. Explain that they should attempt an answer even if they do not fully understand the prompt you have read out. They are not allowed to ask you questions during the game. Also explain that if they are unable to think of an ending or write down their answer in time, they should go on to the next prompt as soon as you start reading it.
Possible prompts: (Adapt to the knowledge of your class.)

1. *The thief admitted ...*
2. *What time did you arrange ...*
3. *The doctor told me to give up ...*
4. *My boyfriend denied ...*
5. *I was so tired I decided not ...*
6. *I'm really tired. Can you help me ...*
7. *The old tramp imagined ...*
8. *I'm sorry but the doctor is busy. Do you mind ...*
9. *I'm very happy at the moment because I'm learning ...*
10. *It was raining very hard so I postponed ...*
11. *I need to practise ...*
12. *I've got so little money I can't manage ...*
13. *The food in the restaurant was so bad the manager offered ...*
14. *He was bored so I suggested ...*
15. *You're horrible. Don't pretend ...*
16. *My teacher got really angry and threatened ...*

CATEGORIES 2

Look at these verbs. Some of them are followed by the -ing form and some of them are followed by the to infinitive. Write a sentence putting them in the correct column. Use the words in the box and begin each sentence with I.

refuse · enjoy · can't afford · expect
promise · feel like · can't help · hope
avoid · keep on · want · miss

go to work · write to you · get out without him seeing me · stay in bed · find a job soon · stay here
see that film · go on the roads · snore · go for a swim · move · make the same mistake

-ing form
I enjoy staying in bed.

to infinitive
I refuse to move.

PICTURE STORY

Relative Clauses (Non-defining): *Juliette, whose boyfriend Masim is always late, was waiting outside the church at 11 o'clock, when the wedding was to take place.*

Divide the class into teams of two to three players and appoint team secretaries. Go through the example with the whole class. Point out how the different relative pronouns are used: *who* for people, *which* for things, *whose* for possession, *where* for places and *when* for time.

The team secretaries, helped by the rest of the team, then have to complete the story of the disastrous wedding. The first team to do this correctly is the winner.

> ANSWERS: Juliette, whose boyfriend Masim is always late, was waiting outside the church at 11 o'clock, when the wedding was to take place. She was just about to go home when she saw Masim, whose watch had stopped, running down the road.
>
> Then Masim's friend Dave, who was supposed to take photographs of the wedding, had forgotten to buy a film. Juliette also got very angry because her cousin Lucy, whose boyfriend is very jealous, smiled a lot at Masim.
>
> Afterwards everybody went to the Duke Hotel, where the wedding reception took place. The staff at the hotel were very unfriendly and the wedding cake, which had cost a lot of money, was stale.
>
> Juliette's father, who was paying for the reception, got very angry and complained to the manager. The manager asked him to go into the lobby of the hotel, where two security guards threw him out.
>
> Juliette's best friend, Chiara, only arrived at 5 o'clock, when the wedding reception was over and everybody was outside the hotel. Then Chiara, who works in a travel agent's, found she had forgotten Masim and Juliette's airline tickets to the Canary Islands, where they were going to have their honeymoon.
>
> Chiara ran to a telephone box to ask Kostos, who is her boss, to send the tickets by taxi to the airport. Then Masim and Juliette got into their car and said goodbye to everybody. But the car, which they had hired for the wedding, wouldn't start and they had to catch a bus to the airport.

GENERAL KNOWLEDGE QUIZ

Relative Clauses (Non-defining): *John Lennon, who was born in Liverpool in 1945, wrote many famous songs.*

Prepare a list of statements concerning general knowledge. This list should suit the cultural standpoint of your students. Divide the class into teams of two to three players and appoint team secretaries. Then write your statements in jumbled order as three lists on the board. For example:

1 John Lennon	is best known for his comic character of the little tramp	died when she was 14.
2 Anne Frank	wrote the Diary of a Young Girl	directed most of his films himself.
3 Charlie Chaplin	was born in Liverpool in 1945	wrote many famous songs.

The team secretaries, helped by the rest of their team, then write sentences joining the facts together using non-defining relative clauses. For example:

> 1 John Lennon, who was born in Liverpool in 1945, wrote many famous songs.

The first team to do this correctly is the winner.
The quiz could be prepared in categories such as *famous people*, *places*, *animals*. Ensure that all relative pronouns are practised. For example:

> *The Tower of London, which was built as a fortress and prison, is one of London's most popular tourist attractions.*

> *The Alhambra, where you can wander in many beautiful gardens and courtyards, overlooks the city of Granada.*

> *February, when the Carnival takes place, is the time of the year when Rio is most crowded.*

PICTURE STORY

Look at these pictures from last week's episode of a TV soap called *Londoners*. The episode was about a disastrous wedding. Put the pictures in the right order and then complete the story. Use *who, which, whose, where, when* and the words in the box.

1. Juliette, whose boyfriend Masim is always late, was waiting outside the church at 11 o'clock, when the wedding was to take place. She was just about to go home when she saw Masim, ..., running down the road.

Juliette's father, ..., got very angry and complained to the manager. The manager asked him to go into the lobby of the hotel, ...

Juliette's best friend, Chiara, only arrived at 5 o'clock, ... Then Chiara ...., found she had forgotten Masim and Juliette's airline tickets to the Canary Islands, ...

Chiara ran to a telephone box to ask Kostos, ..., to send the tickets by taxi to the airport. Then Masim and Juliette got into their car and said goodbye to everybody. But the car ...., wouldn't start and they had to catch a bus to the airport.

Afterwards everybody went to the Duke Hotel, ... The staff at the hotel were very unfriendly and the wedding cake, ..., was stale.

Then Masim's friend Dave, ..., had forgotten to buy a film. Juliette also got very angry because her cousin Lucy, ..., smiled a lot at Masim.

---

watch had stopped   the wedding reception took place   boyfriend Masim is always late

they were going to have their honeymoon   works in a travel agent's

two security guards threw him out   was paying for the reception   they had hired for the wedding

the wedding reception was over and everybody was outside the hotel

was supposed to take photographs of the wedding   is her boss

boyfriend is very jealous   had cost a lot of money   the wedding was to take place

MEMORY 8

Reported Speech (Questions): *She asked him if he had packed the tin opener.*

Photocopy pages 79 and 94 to play this game.

Divide the class into teams of two to three players and appoint team secretaries. Hand out page 79 and give the teams five minutes to study and memorise the picture. Then get the teams to cover or hand you back page 79. Hand out page 94 and go through the examples with the whole class. Point out the two different types of reported questions: *asked/wanted to know if ...* for direct questions (questions that don't have a question word) and *asked/wanted to know* + question word for indirect questions (questions that begin with a question word).

The team secretaries, helped by the rest of their team, then write down what questions the different people asked at the holiday camp. Set a fifteen-minute time limit for them to complete the sentences. They must not look back at the first page while doing this. The team with the most correct sentences is the winner.

ANSWERS:

C She asked what they had been eating.
D He wanted to know if she cried at night.
E He asked her if it was safe to swim in the sea.
F She asked him what he had said.
G She wanted to know where she could get some water.
H He asked her what she was listening to.
I He wanted to know how long dinner would be.
J He asked him if he had locked the car.
K He wanted to know if she had any matches.
L She asked him if he was going to the disco that night.
M She asked her if she would pass her the knife.

LONG SENTENCE GAME

Reported Questions: *She asked me how I was.*

Begin the game by asking the nearest player to you a question, for example, *How are you today?* Explain that this player has to report your question to the next player and then ask him or her a new question, for example, *She asked me how I was. Did you have a good time last night?* The game continues with each player in turn trying to remember what the last player said and then adding a new question to the list. Players get a minus point if they (*a*) make a memory mistake; (*b*) hesitate too long. Do not give players minus points for grammar mistakes – just correct the mistake and let the next player continue. Encourage a mix of direct and indirect questions. Example round:

Player 1: *She asked me how I was. Did you have a good time last night?*

Player 2: *She asked him how he was. He asked me if I'd had a good time last night. What's your favourite food?*

Player 3: *She asked him how he was. He asked her if ...* (This player hesitates too long and so gets a minus point.)

Player 4: (continues) *She asked him how he was. He asked her if she'd had a good time last night. She asked him what his favourite food was. Do you like watching soaps on TV?*

Player 5: *She asked him how he was. He asked her if she'd had a good time last night. She asked him what his favourite soap was.*
(This player makes a memory mistake and so gets a minus point.)
And so on.

At the end, the player with the least number of minus points is the winner.

Hints: Play a trial round before playing for real.

Who is asking what? Write the letters (A-M) in the correct speech balloons.

Then try to memorise what each person says. You have five minutes.

- **A.** DID YOU PACK THE TIN OPENER?
- **B.** WHAT TIME DOES THE SHOP OPEN?
- **C.** WHAT HAVE YOU BEEN EATING?
- **D.** DOES SHE CRY AT NIGHT?
- **E.** IS IT SAFE TO SWIM IN THE SEA?
- **F.** WHAT DID YOU SAY?
- **G.** WHERE CAN I GET SOME WATER?
- **H.** WHAT ARE YOU LISTENING TO?
- **I.** HOW LONG WILL DINNER BE?
- **J.** HAVE YOU LOCKED THE CAR?
- **K.** HAVE YOU GOT ANY MATCHES?
- **L.** ARE YOU GOING TO THE DISCO TONIGHT?
- **M.** WILL YOU PASS ME THE KNIFE?

NOW LOOK AT THE SECOND PAGE.

© Macmillan Publishers Limited 1998.

OBSERVATION 6

Wish + Past Perfect: *I wish I had put on different shoes.*

Go through the examples with the whole class. Then divide the class into teams of two to three players and appoint team secretaries. Set a ten-minute time limit for the team secretaries, helped by the rest of the team, to complete the sentences with *wish* and the past perfect of the verbs in the top part of the box and the phrases in the bottom part of the box. The team with the most correct sentences is the winner.

ANSWERS:

3. I wish I hadn't forgotten my umbrella.
4. I wish I had caught that bus.
5. I wish I hadn't bought so much shopping.
6. I wish I had seen a different film.
7. I wish I hadn't quarrelled with my boyfriend.
8. I wish I had eaten in a different restaurant.
9. I wish I hadn't driven so fast.

INVENTION GAME

Wish/If only + Past Perfect: *I wish I hadn't eaten so much.*

Prepare a list of prompts connected to health and ailments to elicit *wish/if only* + past perfect, for example: *I've got stomachache*. Then elicit from the class what appropriate regret the speaker could then express, for example:

I've got stomachache. I wish I hadn't eaten so much.
If only I hadn't drunk all that apple juice.

Divide the class into teams of two to three players and appoint team secretaries. Explain that you are going to read out prompts and that the teams have to write appropriate regrets using *I wish* + past perfect or *If only I* + past perfect.

Read out the prompts. Set a time limit of two minutes after each one for the teams to discuss and for the team secretaries to write down their answers. Explain that they should attempt an answer even if they do not fully understand the prompt you have read out. They are not allowed to ask you questions during the game. Also explain that if they are unable to find an explanation or write down their answer in time, they should go on to the next prompt as soon as you start reading it.

Possible situations: (Adapt to the knowledge of your class.)

1. I've got a headache.
2. I've got very bad sunburn.
3. I've hurt my back.
4. I've got a bad cold.
5. I've got a sore throat.
6. I've cut my finger badly.
7. I've sprained my ankle.
8. I've burnt myself.
9. I've damaged my hearing.
10. I've got a hangover.

OBSERVATION 6

Look at this picture of a street. Nine people in the street are wishing something. What are they thinking?

Use these words:								
buy	catch	drive	eat	forget	quarrel	park	put on	see
in a different restaurant		my umbrella		different shoes		on the pavement		
so fast		so much shopping		that bus		with my boyfriend		a different film

1. I wish I had put on different shoes.
2. I wish I hadn't parked on the pavement.
3. ......
4. ......
5. ......
6. ......
7. ......
8. ......
9. ......

© Macmillan Publishers Limited 1998.

PHOTOCOPIABLE

MEMORY 9

Unreal Past Conditionals (Third Conditional):
If she had cooked the chicken more, she wouldn't have got food poisoning.

Photocopy pages 83 and 95 to play this game.

Divide the class into teams of two to three players and appoint team secretaries. Hand out page 83 and give the teams two minutes to study and memorise the picture. Then get the teams to cover or hand you back page 83. Hand out page 95 and go through the example with the whole class. Point out the structure of the sentence: *If + past perfect + would(n't) have + past participle*. The team secretaries, helped by the rest of their team, then write down how the people could have avoided what happened to them. Set a ten-minute time limit for them to complete the sentences. They must not look back at the first page while doing this. The team with the most correct sentences is the winner.

> ANSWERS:
> 2. If he hadn't stood on the chair he wouldn't have broken his arm.
> 3. If she had worn her seatbelt she wouldn't have injured her neck.
> 4. If she had read the instructions, she wouldn't have burnt her hand.
> 5. If he hadn't got into a fight, he wouldn't have got a black eye.
> 6. If he had looked at what he was doing, he wouldn't have cut his finger.
> 7. If she had gone down the steps, she wouldn't have sprained her ankle.
> 8. If he hadn't climbed up the fence, he wouldn't have bruised his leg.

I REGRET ...

Unreal Past Conditionals (Third Conditional):
Of course, if I hadn't taken the money, I would still be a minister.

Prepare a number of short, invented speeches that famous people (both living and dead) and fictitious and mythological characters could have said regretting actions they have done in the past. Go though a few examples with the whole class, for example, a politician who has been recently exposed in the press for taking a bribe: *Of course, if I hadn't taken the money, I would still be a minister. But if that stupid man hadn't told the journalists everything, nobody would have found out.* Elicit from the class what the name of the person is.

Divide the class into teams of two to three players and appoint team secretaries. Then read out the speeches. Set a time limit of two minutes after each one for the teams to discuss and for the team secretaries to write down their ideas. Explain that they should attempt an answer even if they are not sure who the famous person is. They are not allowed to ask you questions during the game. Example speeches:

> *If I'd stayed with the band, I'd be rich and famous now. I wouldn't have left if we hadn't had a fight about the kind of music we were playing at the time. (a musician who left a band which later became very famous)*

> *If I hadn't moved away from the goal-line, I would have been able to stop them scoring. We'd have won the league if I hadn't made that one mistake. (a goalkeeper recently in the news)*

> *Of course, if I hadn't thought so much about things, everything wouldn't have ended so badly. Perhaps it would have been better if I'd stayed at university in Germany and not gone back to Denmark. (Hamlet)*

You could play a further round of the game with speeches written by the students.

Look at this hospital casualty ward. Find these people:

- someone who has food poisoning
- someone who has broken their arm
- someone who has injured their neck
- someone who has burnt their hand
- someone who has got a black eye
- someone who has cut their finger
- someone who has sprained their ankle
- someone who has bruised their leg

You have two minutes to memorise who has what.

NOW LOOK AT THE SECOND PAGE.

PRONUNCIATION

Pronunciation

Story telling
Ask a player to begin reading the story about Lewis Carroll. As soon as the player makes a mistake in his or her reading (for example, by pausing after *beginning a conversation* as though there should be a full-stop there), stop the reading and ask another player to take over, starting from the beginning of the story once more. Continue in this way until the story has been successfully read by a player.

Then get the players to punctuate the story according to how it was finally read.

Hints: You could extend this game by taking texts and writing them out without any punctuation and capital letters. (Long monologues from plays make ideal material for this.) The texts are then passed around from player to player as above.

Silent letters
Working individually or in pairs, the players spell the words illustrated in the pictures.

Rhyming twins
Working individually or in pairs, the players match two words which have the same rhyme.

ANSWERS:

Story telling
The English writer, Lewis Carroll, loved making friends with children. He always tried to think of original and funny ways of beginning a conversation with any child he happened to meet. One day Carroll was writing a letter by the sea when a little girl ran past him. The girl had been swimming in the sea and was completely wet from head to foot, dripping water everywhere she walked. Carroll saw the little girl, quietly picked up his sheet of blotting paper and tore off a very small corner. He then held the corner out to the little girl and asked her whether she would like to dry herself with it.

Silent letters
2. queue; 3. wrist; 4. knitting; 5. lightning; 6. lamb; 7. knife; 8. cushion

Rhyming twins
white – night; rough – stuff; raw – door; so – sew; cheap – sleep; sail – tale; half – laugh; aunt – plant; thought – caught; sun – ton; eat – meet; own – alone; home – comb; bean – been; new – view; backs – tax; seem – team; penny – any; learn – turn; hour – flower; wear – air; crowd – loud; noise – boys

---

RHYMING COUPLETS

Pronunciation

Write up the word *high* on the board. Divide the class into teams of three to four players. Appoint team secretaries.

The team secretaries, helped by the rest of their team, write down as many words as they can think of which rhyme with *high* – *my, die, lie, sigh, cry, why*, etc. Set a two-minute time limit.

The teams then read out their lists of words. The team secretaries should cross out any duplicate words on their lists which are read out by other teams. At the end, the team with the most words left is the winner. (Check that all the words do rhyme with *high*.)

Play other rounds with different starters, e.g. *tough, how, town, been, no, tower, jet, sat, sit, farm, zoo*.

VOTING GAME

Pronunciation

You will need lists of minimal pairs for this game. The minimal pairs you choose should reflect the sound distinction problems that your class has. For example: *heel/hill, sheep/ship, sit/seat, feet/fit, chip/cheap*. Give the class examples of the two sounds you are going to contrast. The long 'ee' sound of *heel* and the short 'i' sound of *hill*.

Ask each player to write *EE* and *I* in large capital letters, separately, on two pieces of paper.

Explain that you are going to read out pairs of words which sound alike but in fact have two separate sounds, and that after each single word the players should vote on whether it has the long *EE* or the short *I* sound by holding up the appropriate piece of paper. The players should vote in unison and not look at what the others are doing before deciding. Players are out if they (*a*) hold up the wrong letter(s); or (*b*) hesitate too long. Begin to read out the word pairs pausing after each word for the players to vote on which sound the word contains.

The last player left in is the winner. Play further rounds with other minimal pairs.

 # PRONUNCIATION

Story telling
You will find this story difficult to read because it has no punctuation. Try to read it aloud so that it makes sense to you. Then write the story putting in punctuation and capital letters.

For example: The English writer, Lewis Carroll, loved making friends with children. He ...

the english writer lewis carroll loved making friends with children he always tried to think of original and funny ways of beginning a conversation with any child he happened to meet one day carroll was writing a letter by the sea when a little girl ran past him the girl had been swimming in the sea and was completely wet from head to foot dripping water everywhere she walked carroll saw the little girl quietly picked up his sheet of blotting paper and tore off a very small corner he then held the corner out to the little girl and asked her whether she would like to dry herself with it

....
....
....
....
....
....
....
....
....

Silent letters
All these words have silent letters (letters which are not pronounced). Can you spell them?

1. Comb
2. ....
3. ....
4. ....
5. ....
6. ....
7. ....
8. ....

Rhyming twins
Find a 'rhyming twin' in the box for each of these words.

1. through	too	9. aunt	....	17. backs	....
2. white	....	10. thought	....	18. seem	....
3. rough	....	11. sun	....	19. penny	....
4. raw	....	12. eat	....	20. learn	....
5. so	....	13. own	....	21. hour	....
6. cheap	....	14. home	....	22. wear	....
7. sail	....	15. bean	....	23. crowd	....
8. half	....	16. new	....	24. noise	....

| stuff | night | tax | turn | team | door | laugh | meet | plant | alone | any | sleep | loud |
| too | been | caught | air | tale | view | sew | comb | flower | boys | ton | | |

© Macmillan Publishers Limited 1998.   85

MEMORY 1

Now complete the story. Use the verbs in brackets.

It ..**was getting**.... (got/was getting/had got) dark when Manolo got out of school. He ..**stopped**.... (stopped/was stopping/has stopped) on top of the steps to speak to a friend. But then he .... (noticed/was noticing/had noticed) his school bus at the bus stop across the road. He quickly .... (said/was saying/had said) goodbye to his friend and .... (ran/was running/had run) down the steps and across the road.

There was a lot of traffic and by the time he........................ (got/was getting/had got) to the other side of the street, the bus .... (left/was leaving/had left). He .... (missed/was missing/had missed) his bus and there wasn't another bus to his village for two hours. Manolo .... (looked/was looking/had looked) at his watch: it was five to six and his parents .... (expected/were expecting/had expected) him home at seven. He was sure they would be very angry. He ....(had/was having/had had) to get home somehow by seven.

Then he .... (had/was having/had had) an idea. There was a market a few hundred metres down the road which .... (finished/was finishing/had finished) at six. There would be a lot of lorries leaving the market and going down the main coast road past his village.

When Manolo got to the market, a lorry .... (pulled/was pulling/had pulled) out of the entrance. Manolo couldn't believe his luck; it was going to Rosario, a small town just past his village. There was no time to speak to the driver. Manolo .... (climbed/was climbing/had climbed) into the back as the lorry .... (stopped/was stopping/had stopped) at the edge of the road to let some cars past.

Manolo was in the lorry and he was on his way home. When Manolo .... (sat/was sitting/had sat) down on the floor of the lorry, he .... (had/was having/had had) a big shock. He .... (didn't sit/wasn't sitting/hadn't sat) on the floor, he .... (sat/was sitting/had sat) on something very soft. He .... (looked/was looking/had looked) down. It was a large pig. The lorry was full of pigs.

When Manolo .... (jumped/was jumping/had jumped) off the lorry in his village, the school bus .... (didn't arrive/ wasn't arriving/hadn't arrived). Some parents .... (waited/ were waiting/had waited) at the bus stop for their children.

Manolo ran up the hill to his house. When he .... (opened/ was opening/had opened) the door, his parents .... (sat/ were sitting/had sat) at the table. They .... (smiled/ were smiling/had smiled) when they saw their son. 'You're early, Manolo,' his father .... (said/was saying/had said). 'Yes,' replied Manolo, 'but I'm afraid I'm also a bit smelly.'

Complete the sentences. Use *'ll/won't be* + the verbs in brackets.

1. You **won't be sitting** (sit) at your desk in **the office**.
2. You **'ll be sitting** (sit) outside on the terrace of **your hotel**.
3. It .... (rain).
4. The sun .... (shine).
5. You .... (have) a delicious ....
6. You .... (drink) fresh ....
7. You .... (wear) a business ....
8. You .... (wear) a beachrobe and ....
9. You .... (think) about problems at ....
10. You .... (watch) people .... in the pool.
11. You .... (plan) what beautiful .... to visit.
12. You .... (enjoy) yourself.

The young people are looking at a photograph taken of their camping holiday. Write what they were doing. Do not look at the first page again until you have finished. Use these words and *herself/himself* where necessary.

dress	dry	feel	help	look at	relax	shave	wash
behind a tree		in a mirror		in a stream	sick		to some sausages
	under a tree		with a towel			with an electric razor	

1. She was looking at herself in a mirror.
2. He was washing in a stream.
3.
4.
5.
6.
7.
8.

CAN YOU REMEMBER YOUR NEW IDENTITY? COMPLETE THE SENTENCES USING THE CORRECT FORM OF THE VERBS IN BRACKETS.

1. I ....was born in Sydney,........................ Australia. (born)
2. I .... old. (be)
3. My .... doctor. (be)
4. I .... brother. (have got)
5. I .... when I .... (move; be)
6. I .... there. (go to)
7. I .... at the .... (study)
8. I .... years. (be)
9. I .... studies. (finish)
10. I .... restaurant. (work)

11. I .... there for .... (be)
12. My last .... (be)
13. I .... there for .... (work)
14. I .... at the moment. (have got)

15. I .... called .... (stay)
16. I .... for .... (know)
17. I .... at the moment. (take)

18. I .... so far. (have)
19. I .... food. (like)

© Macmillan Publishers Limited 1998.

Use these words: clean her car, shop, wait for a bus for over half an hour, jog, mend his motorbike, help her, write graffiti on the wall, travel all day, swim

1. Why was the little girl's hair wet?
Because she had been swimming.

2. Why did she give the boy some money?
....

3. Why did she have all those bags?
....

4. Why were they sweating?
....

5. Why did the policeman arrest the boy?
....

6. Why were his hands so dirty?
....

7. Why were they so angry?
....

8. Why were they so tired?
....

9. Why was there water on the ground?
....

NOW SAY WHAT YOU SAW. DON'T LOOK AT THE FIRST PAGE AGAIN UNTIL YOU HAVE FINISHED.

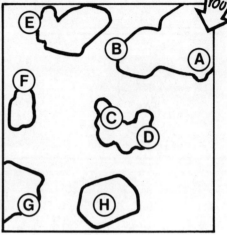

Put a ✓ in the box next to the correct answer.

1. You (A)
    had just got on the bus. ☐
    were just getting on the bus. ☐
    were just going to get on the bus. ☐

2. A car (B)
    had just overtaken the bus. ☐
    was just overtaking the bus. ☐
    was just going to overtake the bus. ☐

3. A cyclist (C)
    had just overtaken the bus. ☐
    was just overtaking the bus. ☐
    was just going to overtake the bus. ☐

4. An old lady (D)
    had just crossed the road. ☐
    was just crossing the road. ☐
    was just going to cross the road. ☐

5. A man (E)
    had just parked his car. ☐
    was just parking his car. ☐
    was just going to park his car. ☐

6. Two children (F)
    had just crossed the road. ☐
    were just crossing the road. ☐
    were just going to cross the road. ☐

7. A woman (G)
    had just got out of the car. ☐
    was just getting out of the car. ☐
    was just going to get out of the car. ☐

8. A van (H)
    had just turned left. ☐
    was just turning left. ☐
    was just going to turn left. ☐

© Macmillan Publishers Limited 1998.

WHAT DID THE PEOPLE AT THE AIRPORT SAY TO EACH OTHER?

A. The announcement said all passengers to Lagos *should go immediately to Gate Five.*

B. The stewardess said they ....

C. The passenger said he ....

D. The young man reminded her not ....

E. The man with the beard said ....

F. The security officer told him to ....

G. The wife said they ....

H. The girl explained that she ....

I. The mother said the plane ....

J. The man with the rucksack told him ....

K. The young man said he ....

L. The old man said he ....

M. The husband said he ....

A. She asked him if he had packed the tin-opener.

B. He wanted to know what time the shop opened.

C. She asked ....

D. He wanted to know ....

E. He asked ....

F. She asked ....

G. She wanted to know ....

H. He asked ....

I. He wanted to know ....

J. He asked ....

K. He wanted to know ....

L. She asked ....

M. She asked ....

INDEX OF STRUCTURE AND LANGUAGE POINTS

Adjectives		freezing, cool, boiling.	8
		(describing people) old, heavy, slim.	8, 38
		(describing objects) It has got a long stick.	8
Adverbs	(comparison)	You won't pass the examination unless you work harder.	42
	(of frequency)	Have you ever been to New York?	56
	(of manner)	'Shut up!' she said angrily.	18
Compound Nouns		a traffic jam.	22
Conditional	(unreal past)	If she had cooked the chicken more, she wouldn't have got food poisoning.	82
Conjunctions		It rained very much during the night.	42
Could have done/been doing		The cats could have had very poor eyesight.	72
Countable Nouns		There aren't as many stamps.	10
Future Continuous		You won't be sitting at your desk in the office.	32
Going to	(future)	I'm going to post these letters.	26
	(decisions)	You're going to travel to Paris.	26
Have something done		He's having his hair dyed.	60
If only	(+ past perfect)	If only I hadn't eaten so much.	80, 82
Imperative		Keep straight on. Don't overtake yet.	6
More/as many/as much		There are more envelopes.	10
Must have done		He must have hidden in the cupboard or in the chest.	72
Nouns (countable/uncountable)		There aren't as many stamps. There isn't as much paper.	10
Participle Adjectives (*-ing* and *-ed*)		The book was very interesting. I'm bored.	28
Passive	(present perfect)	The front door has been mended.	52
	(past perfect)	Rock 'n' roll hadn't been thought of yet.	62
Past Continuous		It was getting dark.	24, 40, 54
Past Perfect Continuous		Because she had been swimming.	24, 50
Past Perfect Simple		Somebody had turned on the TV.	14, 24, 54
Past Simple		It took him weeks to grow.	16, 24, 46
Phrasal Verbs		Who is Danny going out with?	64
Prepositions	(after adjectives)	I'm afraid of spiders.	48
	(of movement)	Who is falling into the lake?	20
Present Continuous		Who is falling into the lake?	20, 40, 46
Present Perfect Simple		I've lost my car keys.	16, 46
Present Simple		I work in a fast food restaurant in Los Angeles.	46
Pronunciation			84
Reflexive Pronouns		She was looking at herself in a mirror.	40
Relative Clauses (defining)		A teetotaller is someone who never drinks alcohol.	34
Relative Clauses (non-defining)		Juliette, whose boyfriend Masim is always late, was waiting ...	34, 76
Reported Speech	(statements)	The announcement said all passengers should go to Gate Five.	58
	(questions)	She asked him if he had packed the tin opener.	78
Should(n't) have done		He should have cleaned his rifle.	70
Uncountable Nouns		There isn't as much paper.	10
Verb	(+ *-ing*)	I enjoy staying in bed.	74
	(+ prepositions)	I think I'm going to apply for this job.	30
	(+ *to* infinitive)	I refuse to move.	74
Vocabulary (verbs)		Don't go in there. Come here.	44
	(American and British)	car, automobile.	68
Want+object pronouns+*to* infinitive		She wants him to buy her an ice cream.	12
Was going to		Someone was going to shave.	36, 54
Will	(future)	Don't worry, I'll answer it.	26
	(decisions)	I know what I'll do! I'll hitch a lift.	26
Wish	(+ past perfect)	I wish I had put on different shoes.	80
Word Order			42, 56